Hockey Showdown

Hockey Showdown

The Canada-Russia Hockey Series

The Inside Story by
Harry Sinden

1972
Doubleday Canada Ltd., Toronto, Ontario
Doubleday & Company, Inc., Garden City, N.Y.

Dedication
To my colleagues on Team Five . . . for their indomitable spirit.
And to our gallant 31-man crew . . . for rowing us ashore.

Library of Congress Catalog Card Number 72-94372

Copyright © 1972 by Harry Sinden
All rights reserved
Printed in Canada
First Edition
ISBN (hardbound) 0-385-04454-2
        (paperback) 0-385-04463-1
Design/Peter Maher

Contents

CONTENTS Continued

Acknowledgment
This book would not have been possible without the assistance
of Will McDonough, sportswriter for The Boston Globe and a
long time personal friend. It was his idea, at the formation of
Team Canada, for a diary which would serve as an accurate
record of this unprecedented series. He told me what to look
for, how to record it; then put it together. He was my guide for
every word.

   None of it would have been possible without the assistance
of my wife Eleanor, who gave me great strength with her
courage and her conviction that my participation was needed
as head coach and general manager of Team Canada. From
the day I was given the assignment until the day we left Russia,
she served as both mother and father to our four daughters, so
that I would be able to have a total commitment to the task at
hand.

Preface

Just as the first Sputnik opened the heavens, our series with the Soviets—the first International World Series of hockey—will propel our game to unlimited heights in the future.

Hockey has been the Canadian game. We fostered it, loved it, nurtured it, thought it would be ours forever. This series showed that there are many nations now who want to share this great game with us at its top level of excellence. We should feel proud of this, not threatened by it. We should feel we have groomed a beautiful child whom the rest of the world wants to love with us. For years, the Russians, Czechs, Swedes and others studied our game and the way we developed it. They have learned their lessons well. Now it's time for us to learn a few from them—especially from the Soviets, who I feel have invented new methods which transcend some of those that are still an integral part of the Canadian style.

In the future, the interests of hockey will be best served by a legitimate "World Series," matching the best from North America against the best from Europe. The greatest hockey I have ever witnessed was played during our Team Canada-Russia series. It was unmatched in the annals of the game for continuous action. The Russians pushed us to the limit, but at the same time we induced the Soviets to bring their game to a peak. My feeling is that the Russians so dominated international play, they were never forced to display all their great skills until we became the challenge. I salute the Soviet players, and their coaches, for their dedication to the game. In many ways, they are, right now, the best players in the world.

But for the present, I'll take the players from Team Canada, who staged one of the greatest sports comebacks ever, under extremely trying conditions. As a team we were given the task of winning all eight games. We couldn't. We were asked to endure some questionable tactics on the part of our opponents and the referees, the defection of many of our supporters, and four of our own members, in our hour of need. We did and we won. Some criticized our methods, but the results will be written into history.

Harry Sinden, Oct. 15, 1972.

Hockey Showdown

1
Game One

I wanted to show the Team Canada players how it feels to be playing for your country—that peculiar kind of exhilaration you experience when you're a world champion. But I was apprehensive about how they might take it. I didn't want them to think I was shilling for myself, or taking an ego trip on their time.

My motive was pure. I wanted them to experience my emotions of 14 years ago. I wanted them to relive with me on film those beautiful moments when I stood on top of the world. The summit that day was in Oslo, Norway, where as Captain of the Canadian Hockey team I had just stepped up to accept the World Cup.

Moments before, on an outdoor rink in 12 degree temperatures, we had struck a blow for Canada, the foremost hockey nation in the world. We had beaten the Russians in the final 4 to 2, and avenged losses the Canadian team had suffered at the hands of the Soviets the two previous years.

We regained our pride that day, but a lot has changed since then. We're down to just 48 hours before the opening

1

game of what is being billed as the International World Series of Hockey—Canada and Russia head to head for eight games.

Tonight was my first shot at psyching the team. This was just our 15th day of practice, and I had made sure that all that went on before was strictly physical. This film session was supposed to be mental, the first step we would use to get the guys sky high for Saturday night.

But if anything, it backfired. My players, most of whom were pee-wees when I captained the Whitby-Dunlop team in 1958, thought the whole thing was funny.

I had the entire team watch the movie of that 1958 World Championship game, and two video tapes of the Russian team in recent action. But there, in the press room at Maple Leaf Gardens, the players had a hard time containing their laughter when my picture flickered into focus during the presentation ceremony.

"Who's that little kid with the hat?" needled Phil Esposito.

"Coach, you look like Charlie Chaplin," another player added out of the darkness.

I could laugh at myself now and enjoy it. As I looked at the films—which were poor by modern standards, black and white with no particular continuity—I realized I did look sort of ridiculous. I was 34 when I started coaching with the Boston Bruins in the NHL and on my first trip around the league I was stopped from going to the bench in three different cities because I looked so young. The ushers wouldn't believe I was the coach.

I was 26 when we won in Oslo, and so proud. All Canada had wanted us to hang one on the Russians that day and we did. In 1972 the nation wants it again and it's my job to make sure this team is ready to do it.

On the ice our team has progressed well. In just two weeks these players from different teams in the NHL have really come together as Team Canada. It's been a good training camp, one that myself and Assistant Coach John Ferguson are proud of.

"It's as good as any training camp I was ever at with Montreal," Fergie told me the other day. That made me feel good because the Canadiens had to be doing something right to win all those Stanley Cups during Ferguson's years.

But the psychological preparation has me worried. These guys are used to playing for money, which has been their incentive for all of their professional lives. The pot of gold that goes with the Stanley Cup has always been their inspiration. Will they give their best now because Canadians want them to beat hell out of the Russians? I don't know. And tonight I couldn't get a good reading. In fact I cut the meeting short because it wasn't going the way I planned.

The two video tapes we had weren't really suitable for what we wanted. One was Czechoslovakia's win over Russia last year in the World Championship. The other showed the Russians beating an aggregation of Canadian pros and amateurs in 1969—the last time the Canadians played Russia.

As we watched the tapes with the sole intent of trying to pick out Russian flaws, we became too critical. We picked apart everything they did. It was getting out of hand. I wanted our guys to gain some confidence from this, but I felt sure if I didn't cut it short we would become overconfident.

So we watched just a couple of periods from those games before I switched to the Oslo film. The effect I wanted here was totally different from that of the video tapes. I wanted our guys, as they watched that game and particularly the award ceremony, to pick up the sense of pride and patriotism our team had that day.

And what a day that was! It's so real in *my* memory that I didn't need any movie to bring it back. To the day I die I'll remember everything about that game—the biggest thing in my life to that point.

The background of that game was a lot like the prelude to this series. In 1954, the first time the Russians ever sent a team to the World Cup, they stunned Canada 7 to 2. It was one of the few times Canada had ever been beaten in international competition. Even though it was a relatively poor team, Canada had been used to sending weak teams and still winning.

That threw our country into a state of shock, and it turned to paranoia when Russia beat Canada in the 1956 Olympics. I still remember vividly how outraged everyone was. In 1957, because of the Russian intervention in the Hungarian Revolution, Canada and the United States refused to send teams to the World Championship.

Then came 1958 and our Whitby team was picked to represent Canada in the World Cup. I was a defenseman and captain. Wren Blair, now general manager of the Minnesota

North Stars, was our manager. They set up the draw so we would meet Russia in the finals. We had won all seven of our previous games and Russia had six wins and a tie as we moved into the championship game.

We were high that day, too high. For two periods we couldn't get ourselves together and only great play by Roy Edwards, our goaltender, kept us in the game. It was 2 to 2 with five minutes to play before we got goals from Bob Attersey and Bus Gagnon.

Blair likes to take credit for the Attersey goal which was the eventual winner. At the time Bob was a budding young Conservative politician and one of the better players on our team. In this game Attersey wasn't going well at all, which prompted Blair to come up behind him on the bench and whisper: "The way you're playing today I'm beginning to doubt your true political convictions."

Blair was indicating he thought Attersey might be a little 'pink,' and when Bob scored on his next shift Blair thought he was a master psychologist.

The end of the game was wild, when 750 Canadian soldiers stationed in Germany came flying into all the excitement. But most of all I remember that beautiful feeling, the goose bumps popping out all over me as I stood on the victory block, the Russian and Swedish captains on either side of me, as our flag went up slowly and they played O Canada.

I hope before this 1972 series is over, these kids can experience that feeling. Money can't buy it. Not even Stanley Cup money.

Montreal, Sept. 1

A funny thing happened in the Forum. Well, I guess 'unusual' is a better word. The Russians arrived and we watched their workout; then they watched ours. I wonder how often that happens—two teams watch each other practice the day before the big game?

The Russians were unimpressive, but they never look good in practice by our standards. In the NHL style of practice the emphasis is on skating and shooting. It has to be. That's our game.

The Russians' is a passing game. When they work out they concentrate on passing and stickhandling. The whole thing is at a very slow and low keyed pace. When I watched them in Oslo in '58 it was this way. When I saw them again at the Olympics in 1960 at Squaw Valley, California, it was just as slow and deliberate.

Our guys just couldn't seem to understand this. After we watched their practice our players were very critical. I kept hearing things like, "The goalie is too deep in the net," or "They can't shoot at all." I tried to stifle those comments. I told the players, "Listen, those guys aren't as bad as they looked."

The Russians also sat around in the Forum for our work out, which, in a way, was doing me a big favor. It was all the incentive our team needed to have a great workout. The players were just like little kids showing off for their parents. We flew all over the ice. And shoot—our guys were unloading all kinds of bombs. I even found myself turning around to take a peek at the Russians' reaction after a guy like Dennis Hull ripped one on the net. It didn't seem to register anything special with them. In fact, they just sat there quietly in a group watching, hardly saying anything to one another. "I'd love to be able to get inside their minds and find out what they really think," I said to myself.

But I was more concerned about my own team today than anything. I had to tell them who was going to dress for the first game here tomorrow night. This is the lousiest job of all for any coach—telling a player, in a sense, he isn't good enough. Because of the novelty of this series, I am in a strange situation. Generally, players that aren't good enough to dress for a big game or even to make a pro team, are fringe players. But how do you tell an All-Star "I'm sorry, but I'm going with so and so instead of you"?

Certainly, when these 35 players came to me two and a half weeks ago, they came with the knowledge that only 19 could dress for each game. Yet, the ones we sit down will be hurt mentally. For many of them, it's undoubtedly going to be the first time in their hockey lives they hear they aren't good enough. Here are kids who have been standouts since pee-wees, great juniors, and now good enough to be All-Stars in the pros. Will they take this in stride? I don't know.

A few of them had their heads down after they saw the list today. I knew that Gilles Perreault and Rick Martin, both from Buffalo, felt a little sorry for themselves. They are both from the Montreal area and were super juniors up here. Naturally, they wanted to come back and turn it on for the home folks. But if two guys weren't going to play here, it was those two. Of the 35 players, Perreault and Martin were the only ones who let down on us in training camp. Neither was playing that well, and after we finished our intra-squad games I could sense that they didn't think they were going to make it. The last week or so they just didn't put out in practice the way they had the first couple of weeks, or the way the other guys had right along.

I did feel badly for Serge Savard, the fine Montreal defenseman. Serge wanted to play here in the worst way, and had worked very hard for the honor. In fairness, though, I didn't think he really came on strong until the last three or four days, and we are going with the guys who earned the shot off what they showed in camp.

John Ferguson and I decided some days ago that we were going to throw an offensive team on the ice against the Russians and carry the play to them. With this in mind, we set up two standards for picking our starting lineup. First, we would dress the players who earned it in training camp. Second, if it's a toss-up among any players, we'll pick the one who fits best into this offensive mold.

The first dozen or so spots were easy. The Ratelle line—Jean Ratelle, Vic Hadfield and Rod Gilbert of the New York Rangers—had been one of the best offensive lines in the history of the NHL and had a pretty good camp. They are one line. The best line in training camp was the one that has Bobby Clarke of Philadelphia centering for Ron Ellis and Paul Henderson of the Toronto Maple Leafs. Then we put together a line with Phil Esposito of the Boston Bruins playing between two other great offensive players, Frank Mahovlich and Yvan Cournoyer. This line should be dynamite.

One important decision that Fergie and I had to reach—we actually did all of this brain picking last night in the hotel after our team meeting in Toronto—was whether to carry a fourth line, or an extra defenseman.

In our negotiations with the Russians, it was agreed we could dress 19 players for each game. Naturally, we had to start with two goaltenders. That meant we could handle the rest of the squad in one of two ways: we could use three lines, two extra forwards and six defensemen, or—and this is what we went for—we could put together four lines and use five defensemen. After weighing all the pros and cons, Fergie and I came to the conclusion that, since we aim to carry the play offensively, we would need extra forwards more than additional defensemen.

We settled on four lines which would contain plenty of guys who are terrific penalty killers. Our fourth line, again put together with offense in mind, had Red Berenson of the Detroit Red Wings centering for teammate Mickey Redmond and Peter Mahovlich of Montreal.

I was worried that we might take a lot of penalties in the first game because our players were bound to be aggressive. So I am satisfied with our selections because we have six good penalty killers in Esposito, Berenson, Ellis, Clarke and Peter and Frank Mahovlich.

We put together our defense this way. Don Awrey of the Bruins and Rod Seiling had been the best pair in training. Awrey complements Seiling with Don's good rugged play and shot blocking, while Rod handles the puck well in his own end and makes the plays coming up ice.

Brad Park, whom we consider to be the premier defenseman on the squad with Bobby Orr hurt, paired well with Gary Bergman in camp. Bergman is a steady, consistent player who can do a job on the power play. I expect this pair to be our best set of offensive defensemen. The fifth defenseman was our toughest pick. We had to take one of six guys who had all played about the same in camp.

We finally decided on Guy Lapointe of Montreal for several reasons. One, he finished up camp playing well. Two, he's an offensive defenseman who can give us some help on the power play if we run into trouble. Three, he's from Montreal and guys generally play their best in front of their home fans, especially in a game like this.

Goaltending also caused some soul searching. If anything, Tony Esposito of the Chicago Black Hawks has a very, very slight edge over Ken Dryden. It's been so close, though, that you can't say Tony should definitely be the starter. Tony would play a starring role one day, Dryden the next. Both have played well.

Dryden is our pick to start. Like Lapointe, we feel that coming back to Montreal will really pick Kenny up. But, if the worst happens, we can come back with Tony in Toronto

Monday night. Really, we're splitting the first two games, and coming back in the third with the guy who does the best job.

After practice, I called the players to center ice and told them that the names of the men who are going to dress for the opener were posted on the bulletin board in the dressing room. I told them what my reasoning was and reminded those who didn't get picked not to be disappointed, because our plan is to play everyone at least once in the series.

The guys accepted this—I feel now, anyhow, the right way. In a situation like this, the players know as well as the coaches who deserves to be picked and who doesn't. I think you get trouble only when you pick someone who doesn't deserve it. Sure, the kids like Perreault, Martin, and Savard hung their heads. It was a blow to their pride. But it would have been a gross injustice to the team for me to play one of them simply because he grew up around here.

Montreal, Sept. 2

A little piece of all of us died today. I've lost some tough games over the years, but I never thought I could feel as badly about losing a single game as I did about this one. Christ, it hurts. The Russians beat us 7 to 3, and almost made fools out of us in the process. The guys who came over to learn something from us professionals gave us a lesson that myself, all our players, and I guess this whole country, won't forget for a long time.

There was no phase of the game at which they didn't outplay us. They skated circles around us and, at the end, they were actually laughing at us. That's the only emotion they showed all night, except when Phil Esposito punched one of them in the face with his glove. The Russian just grinned at Phil as much as to say, "Look at the scoreboard, you jerk."

In all honesty, even though I'm sitting here in a hotel room in Toronto five hours after we were beaten, I can say the loss wasn't totally unexpected. I was afraid it was going to happen, although I never thought they could jolt us like that—7 to 3. I was afraid that they might luck out against us—keep it close and then bang in a crazy goal, a deflection, or something at the last minute when we couldn't do anything about it.

In my heart I rated their chances of beating us one in five. I didn't think they were a better team or had better players.

Even though they beat us handily I still don't know if they are. The next seven games will settle that.

As much as anything, my fear of losing was due to what might be called the embarrassment factor. This is why any coach hates to be an overwhelming favorite like we were. You say to yourself, "Hey, it isn't that much of a cinch!"

You try to fortify yourself in case the unexpected happens. A coach not only prepares his team, somewhere in the deepest recesses of his brain, he also gets himself prepared to lose. I often wonder why these thoughts creep in. I guess it's just human nature. And I don't care who the coach is, or how cocky he acts, unless he's a complete moron he's afraid of losing no matter how big a favorite he is.

My first reaction, once I tried to pull the pieces together, was to blame myself. "I blew it. I blew it," I kept telling myself as we flew to Toronto after the game. But the more I think about it, the more I think I didn't blow it. Neither did the players. We simply got blown off the ice by a fine hockey team that outpositioned us in the beginning and outconditioned us at the end.

The best way to put the game in its proper perspective is to start at the beginning of the day. Saturday we scheduled a light workout at the Forum from noon to 12:30 for the members of the squad who were playing. The rest of the team went to a luncheon.

There was a good feeling at practice. The guys were high and happy as they loosened up. You could see they were a little more chipper than usual, which is a sign to a coach that the adrenalin was already starting to flow, even though the faceoff was eight hours away.

After the skating, we held our final team meeting in the Junior Canadien dressing room, which is right beside the Canadiens' regular dressing room, the one we were going to use for the game. Even though we had discussed our game plan as a group before, I wanted to go over the whole thing once more to eliminate any doubts.

The major elements of our plans were: (1) to put as much offensive pressure on the Russians as we could, (2) to play the exact same style of hockey we played in the NHL; (3) to shoot as often as we could and from any angle because their goaltending was questionable; (4) to be aggressive, but only when we were in position to hit; (5) not to do any fighting.

The players all seemed to agree this was the right approach. Why should we go into the game with a defensive posture when the Russians had to show the Canadians they could play hockey with us?

The reason we formulated the plan we did can be dissected and studied. We wanted to go after them offensively because we felt if we could break fast and hit them with a couple of quick goals they might panic. We wanted to play the NHL style of game because we didn't want to make adjustments that might start our players thinking too much. We just wanted those guys out there doing the things they do naturally. For instance, we wanted our forwards to watch their points in our end; our centers to come back deep in our end to take the short pass coming out; and our center to play about 15 to 20 feet directly out in front of the net—the slot, where Esposito plays so well.

We wanted to shoot a lot, even from bad angles, because we thought their goaltender would be shaky and might blow some easy ones. One thing we didn't want was to go out of our way to hit somebody, even though we wanted aggressiveness. The Russian style thrives on opponents who are out of position.

Finally, we wouldn't fight under any circumstances because we didn't want to get thrown out of the game. I particularly warned the men about getting sucked into a fight. I've seen it happen myself in International play—a European tricks a Canadian into a fight and then walks away. Not only does the Canadian get thrown out, but also his team has to play the next 10 minutes shorthanded. I told the players this policy meant they would have to take a lot more guff than they were used to taking in the NHL, but they said they would do it without retaliating.

A good part of our meeting that afternoon also concerned our power play and what we would do when we were short-handed. On the power play I wanted to get as many shots from the point as we could because they just don't shoot from the point in Europe and I thought their goalie wouldn't be able to handle them as well. And I told them to get those shots up—get them high on him, where he is supposed to be weak.

We set up our penalty killing by trying to break up the Russians in their end before they got started. We didn't want them to get their great passing game started. Our aim was to disorganize them in their end.

At the end of the meeting I asked the players for their suggestions. We had done this throughout training. We wanted the players to have their say and to feel as much a part of the series as anybody, including their coach. But their comments were all general . . . we had to shoot a lot, hit a lot, things like that.

I left that meeting feeling exceptionally good. Even though that fragment of nagging doubt was still someplace in my thoughts, I felt that if we played just an adequate game by our standards there was no way the Russian team could beat us. This feeling was with me throughout the afternoon, and I know the players felt the same way.

The players spent a typical pre-game afternoon. Most of them took a short walk near the hotel. Later they tried to take a nap, but it was probably more of a rest on top of their beds.

Different groups went to the Forum with their cab captain about 90 minutes before the game. I waited a little longer before going to the rink. I do this by design. I don't like to get to the rink more than an hour before the game and I don't like to hang around the dressing room with the players.

When I got there and walked into the room, there was an air of anxiety among the players. They wanted badly to get out on the ice and show everyone how good they were. Even though they had only 17 days of training, even though they were from different teams and hadn't really played that much together, they were confident that their ability was going to make up for anything they were going to face that night. This was an exciting event for them. And me too. I was starting to sweat already, and that usually doesn't happen until the game starts.

I thought at the time, "Why am I this nervous?" And my answer was that I just didn't know how good this Russian team was or what to really expect from it. I was like my players, I wanted the game to start now. Just five minutes. That's all I'd need. Just to see the Russians in action for that long and I'd know whether we were that much better than them and whether we could beat them no matter how we played.

Frankly, I started to be a little afraid at this point. I knew we weren't in the condition they were and I had the feeling maybe . . . maybe we're not quite as good as I thought we were. This is when, about 50 minutes before the game, I felt most afraid of losing.

The first thing I did when I checked into our dressing room

was to get together with our doctors and trainer. If you've ever coached in any sport, you'll know that you're always apprehensive as you arrive at the room on the day of the game. There's always the chance of someone getting sick at the last minute—a virus, some kind of bug, a freak accident.

But everything was fine and I went in briefly to check with the players and let them know I was there. "Just make sure you're getting yourself mentally prepared," I told them. "This is what we've been waiting for and I know you're ready to do the job."

My first appearance in front of the players before a game is always brief. I just try to encourage them and then disappear. I don't want them to see me again until just ten minutes before the faceoff. I think the worst thing a coach can do is stay around the dressing room and talk with the players. Then by the time you get up to tell them what you want them to do, there isn't anything left to say. You can't send them out to play with a little push if you have nothing to say to get them up.

Usually, I go into the coaches' room and stay out of sight. But tonight I was anxious to get a look at the ice, so I went outside. The surface was fresh and looked fast. They had put a couple of floods on it after both teams had practiced. The ice we practiced on in Toronto had been slow, so I felt the good ice would make our guys happy. Every player likes to think he's flying out there.

It was very hot in the Forum and the crowd hadn't come in yet. "How hot is it going to be when 18,000 bodies get in here?" I wondered. The heat will hurt us more than it will them, I thought. When the crowd started coming in I walked back toward the dressing room, but I still didn't want to go in. I stayed outside for a while and the fans were nice, getting autographs and wishing me well. Soon it got too crowded, so I went inside to a small coaches' room and joined John Ferguson to go over our game plan for the final time.

"Don't forget you can use Pete Mahovlich on the power play if you need him, and LaPointe, too," Fergie reminded me, as we doublechecked each other on our strategy. I had told Fergie that I wanted him to keep an eye on the Russians as much as he could. He was going to sit right behind the bench and would have a different perspective than I. And with me following the puck all the time, and our players, I wouldn't have time to pick up everything that the Russians might be doing. I told him to watch especially for any new wrinkles the Russians might try, either on the power play or with their penalty killing. Our meeting lasted about 20 minutes and we could tell by the way we smiled at each other when we finished that we were happy with our plans.

I thought I could spend the next 15 minutes with my own thoughts, attempting to sort out exactly what I wanted to say to the players; but it wasn't to be. The official scorer came over for my lineup and I was anxious to see the Russian lineup. We wanted to open the game with the Ellis-Clarke-Henderson line. This was our fastest group and every game usually opens at a fast pace. But we also wanted them to go up against the best Russian unit—the Kharlamov line.

"They wouldn't give the lineup to me," the scorer said. "I asked them for it and they told me to come over here and get yours first."

This really bugged me. There was no question that we were the home team, and the home team always hands in its lineup last. This was just one of their cute tricks. The Russians knew what they were doing, there was no doubt about that. During our negotiations, they said they wanted the home team to alternate each game. But I told them: "Listen, there isn't any way I'm going to allow a visiting team to be the home team in a Canadian city." So they agreed that we would be the home team for the four games in Canada, and they would be the home team for all the games in Russia.

I tell you, that scorer was a little shook up when I sent him back to the Russians' room. He did get the lineup from them, but they gave him a hard time before handing it over. The scorer wasn't too sure what was what, except that the Kharlamov line wasn't starting. That was all we really wanted to know.

We switched to the Esposito line. This way we could still get the Clarke line on against Kharlamov, which was our main objective with the matching of lines.

See, we really didn't know very much about the Russians except for a few players. They certainly knew a lot more about us. They had their two coaches sitting up in the stands watching everything we did during the past two weeks, taking enough notes to fill an encyclopedia. When they pulled that routine with the scorer I knew what they were up to. They wanted to see if we'd hand in our lineup first so they could match up lines to their satisfaction.

All of this still didn't bother me because another part of me was saying, "Look, what does it all matter? They better look out for us. We shouldn't adjust to them!" I just didn't want them to get away with something that might give them the idea they could get away with anything they liked.

Our team warmed up well. In the midst of the confusion over the lineup I took a peek at what our guys were doing on the ice. I didn't want them to start pumping goals past Ken Dryden instead of giving him the work he needed. The object of the warm-up is to get the goalie ready for shots on any area of the net. He should be getting the feel of the puck. But in the NHL, and other areas of hockey, particularly with kids, the guys go in on the goal and blast away instead of building up their goalie's confidence by giving him the shots that will get him ready.

Dryden was ready. Our players could feel it. When they came back to the room there was plenty of noise and yelling. "Let's hit them and keep hitting them." "Shoot, shoot, shoot!" and shouts like that were bouncing off the walls for three or four minutes.

This banter is part of hockey. It's like group therapy. The players psyche themselves this way. I often thought that this must have been why Indians screamed war cries on the way into battle—a sign that they were all in the thing together.

The room quieted down in a couple of minutes. All the players sat on benches, making last minute repairs to their equipment. When they saw me moving to the middle of the room there was absolute silence. It was kind of eerie. You get the feeling that the first couple of words are going to get stuck in your throat and you'll feel kind of stupid.

Very quickly I went over our pre-game strategy, the same things we discussed at the noon meeting. "Don't forget: We want to play aggressive hockey, but let's not take any foolish penalties," I said. "Shoot, and keep shooting.

"But most of all I want you to remember this. We're going to play this game for Canada. We're going to play it for the people of the country and for hockey, and what it means to this country. And most of all, we're going to play it for ourselves and our own reputations. I want you to think of how hard you worked these last weeks and what you gave up to be here. Now we're laying our reputations on the line for the world to see. That's why I want any benefits that will go with winning this game and this series to go to you. You've earned it."

That's all I had to say. I felt they were extremely high and I didn't want them to go any higher. When my little speech was over, none of the players had anything to say. There wasn't anything left, I guess.

Then Pete Mahovlich, the holler guy on the team, let go with a blast. And that started the rest of the players buzzing. As they got up and started to put on their gloves and grab their sticks, I started around the dressing room to meet with each of them individually.

I didn't plan what happened, but it became very emotional. As I moved along telling each one of them, "Good luck. I hope you perform to the best of your ability,"—I could see clearly that these players—these men who really aren't supposed to care about anything but money—were very touched by this game.

I had never experienced that kind of a feeling with a team before. It wasn't like a Stanley Cup game where "the money on the line" is what the players react to. It was, "I'm playing for the postman, the milkman, and every other Canadian in the world who ever put on skates and thought about being the best in the world, if only in his dreams."

This reaction was a complete surprise to me. I always felt that in order to have a feeling of 'team' among a group of players they must first experience something together. They must win, win a big game when their guts are on the line, when their courage and ability are being questioned.

But tonight that feeling of team was there in that room just before the faceoff for only one reason. They were Russia. We were Canada. They were the new guys on the block and we weren't about to let them take our territory from us.

I was anxious to get to the ice. Our guys were ready for a great effort. On the way to the bench I reminded them that there would be a 25 minute wait during pre-game ceremonies. This type of thing can scramble a player's thoughts if he isn't prepared for it. I didn't want any of them getting fidgety and losing his edge.

Finally, after all the waiting and wondering what it would be like, the faceoff came. In thirty seconds I felt like a genius. We got the puck and took it right into their end. Yvan Cournoyer dug it out of the corner and passed to Frank Mahovlich. Frank got the shot off and Tretiak juggled it. The puck popped into the air and Phil Esposito speared it out of the air with his stick and punched it into the net.

Bedlam. That's the only way to describe it. The building went nuts and so did our bench. I lost my cool and started jumping around like the players. But just as fast I checked myself: "Hey, this is only 30 seconds. We've got 59 more minutes to play!" I had never seen a bench react that wildly to a goal in the first half minute. The last half minute, yes, but not with the rest of the game to play.

When I got myself together, and got the guys to cool it, I decided to change lines. Quite often after a goal like that the line on the ice will have a letdown, and before you know it the other guys are right back for one of their own.

Now a strange thing started to happen. Before the game, I had told anyone who wanted to listen, "Just let me see them on the ice for five minutes and I'll tell you how tough the Russians are."

I was wrong. I needed only three minutes. In the two minutes following Phil's goal the Russians tore up and down the ice making beautiful passes, taking beautiful passes, getting their men in position, outskating us to loose pucks, and doing everything but putting it in the net.

It was right then I knew the Russians were everything I didn't want them to be, and everything we were led to believe they wouldn't be.

Even when we went ahead 2 to 0 at the six minute mark on a nice goal by Paul Henderson, I knew it was going to be a grinder. The only thing we counted on that went right was the faceoffs. The Russians were proving to be weak in this department, as we thought.

On our second goal, Bobby Clarke, a good faceoff man, won the draw and got it to Henderson. Paul got off a good high shot and zipped it past Tretiak. "He isn't that good," I thought. "He's weak on the high shots like they said he would be."

Now I started thinking we could hold on and beat these people if we could get enough good shots at Tretiak, even though they were dominating the puck and filtering through our defense.

I just couldn't believe I was seeing the Russians go around and through us so easily. But they did and got two quick goals on us before the period ended. First, they zipped a pass from behind our net out front and Zemin put it in. Then they got a shorthanded goal on us with something they do very well. They got a two-on-one break and the second guy in, Petrov, followed up the missed shot just like a basketball player would go to the hoop for a rebound, and Petrov put it in.

Our guys set this up by losing their poise. We were running all over the ice because we wanted to prove to the fans, and to the Russians, that we were superior not only in shooting but also in aggressiveness.

By doing this, running at them when there wasn't any need to, we just became perfect opponents for them. We had gone out of our way to establish the hitting part of the game. Left wingers were on right wing trying to hit somebody; defensemen were at the other end throwing their weight around. We were setting a pattern that spelled defeat if we kept it up.

Between periods in the dressing room, I just tried to get everyone calmed down. "Stop running all over the place," I told them. "Just play your own position and let the other guy play his. You can't do this thing all by yourself. First and foremost you have to take care of your own job."

Once I thought that had sunk in, I went back over the faceoffs. This was a weakness in the Russians which I wanted to stress, because I thought it could get us another goal, and because it would give our guys some hope, if any of them were losing it.

The players sat there drenched in perspiration from the heat. I could tell by looking into their eyes that they realized the Russians were very good . . . so good that we couldn't just play any way we wanted and still beat them.

Personally, at this point, I was confused about the Russian style. It seemed to be the same as we watched in the movies, but the game was whirling by me so fast I hadn't picked up anything that could really make a difference.

The only thing that surprised us in the first period—outside of the Russians' great individual ability—was that they were using longer passes than we anticipated. From all our films of them, and from our scouts' reports, it seemed like they played strictly a short passing game. In the first period they showed they could hit you with the long one in a hurry, and they were constantly trying to break a man coming up the middle out of their own end.

I still didn't try to change our defense because I wasn't convinced that we couldn't beat them with the NHL style of play. Maybe it was rationalization (and as I look back now it was) but I believed if our players got back to basics and stopped running around out of position, we would beat them.

One correction we did try to make was the way our defensemen, particularly Don Awrey and Rod Seiling, were dropping down in front of shots only to see the Russians fake the drive and move around them and in on our goaltender.

Bobby Orr, who was sitting in the stands with Eddie Johnston, saw what was happening and came running into the room after the first period. "You've got to get those guys to stop dropping in front of the puck. The Russians don't shoot from out there. We've got to stop," urged Bobby, who was really excited.

Before the game I had asked Eddie Johnston to keep a check on the game and report in with me. Eddie, a keen student of hockey, backed up what John Ferguson and I already knew—we were beating ourselves by not playing solid positional hockey.

The second period verified what we had suspected about Kharlamov. He's a helluva hockey player. He got two goals in that period and gave Russia a 4 to 2 lead.

His first goal was just magnificent. He came into our zone alone against Seiling and Awrey. As he came across the blue line he dipped his left shoulder like he was going to bust to the inside and between them. When Awrey started to go with the move, Kharlamov just blew by him to the outside, and then swooped back in front of the net, still in complete control. As he swept in front of Dryden, Kharlamov made a move as if he was going to switch the puck to his backhand, but all of a sudden he gave it a quick forehand flip into the far corner of the net.

Our players were stunned. I looked down the bench and I caught two of our great offensive players, Esposito and Mahovlich, looking at each other and just shrugging their shoulders as if to say "Can you believe that?"

All of us were impressed but none of us wanted to let on. There were good reasons, too. For one, I've very seldom seen anyone come down on two NHL defensemen and beat them to the outside, going around them and in on the net. It just isn't done.

Secondly, Don Awrey is one of the toughest men in the game to beat to the outside. If you go around Awrey, he just keeps taking you into the boards because he's very quick on his skates. Kharlamov blew past him without getting touched. It was like a piece of cake. All of us wanted to think it was lucky, that it wouldn't happen again. We didn't want to acknowledge how great a play it was.

For some reason we seemed to play better after this. They scored again, but we played our best hockey of the night, even though we came out of the period trailing 4 to 2.

In the dressing room before the third period, I knew I had to make some changes, although I really didn't want to. The Ratelle line was getting beaten badly. Ratelle's unit needed time to move the puck the way it had in the NHL, but the Russians weren't giving it to them. Ratelle's line was on the ice for two of the first three Russian goals, and just didn't get into the flow of the game. Awrey was having a bad night as well. So I decided to bench Awrey in favor of Guy LaPointe and to go with three lines instead of four.

Our plans had to be forgotten. We had wanted four lines against them so that our forwards wouldn't get worn out from pressing the attack. Instead, our defense was being worn down from the constant pressure. We would have been better off going with six defensemen in three pairs.

In view of the heat, and against a team that had superior conditioning I knew that working extra shifts in the third period was a lot to ask from our guys. Because of this, I also warned our players to be cautious, despite the fact that we were two goals down. The biggest thing was not to get blasted out of the game early in the period. I didn't want them to take a defensive posture, yet we couldn't keep gambling with these people and let them run three-on-two breaks all night.

We started the third period the same way we finished the second, playing better. Near the 10 minute mark, Bobby Clarke scored for us to bring it back to 4 to 3. Our guys were wiped out physically, but the idea of being just a goal away kept us playing well.

A few minutes later I thought for an instant we might pull it off. Cournoyer moved in for a great chance and hit the post. The puck bounced away and the game was over in the next 10 seconds. The Russians took the puck back up ice and ripped a shot off the post. The difference was that theirs went into the net. There were still four minutes or so to play, but we were gone. The players had nothing left to give. The Russians could sense this and moved in for the kill. At the end, they put two more goals by Dryden. Maybe this was appropriate, because they were four goals better than we were tonight.

When the clock read five seconds left to play, I walked off the bench to the dressing room. I wanted those few extra moments to collect my thoughts and find the right words to ease the pain when it was time to talk to the players.

They came through the door right behind me, discarding their sticks and peeling off their soggy jerseys as they went.

The next thing we knew Al Eagleson, president of the NHL Players Association, came flying into the room. "Get the players back out there," he yelled. "The Russians are still on the ice waiting to shake hands with us. Get the players."

I rushed into the room and told the guys quickly what was happening. All of them jumped up and started to put their gear back on. As we hit the door, though, we could see the last of the Russians going off the ice. It was too late, and I was really ticked off. No one had ever told me or the players that we were supposed to meet with the Russians on the ice after the game. It's common in international play, but we didn't know until later that the people from Hockey Canada had made this arrangement. When I asked them about it they answered, "Well, we just assumed that you'd know." Those people assume a lot of things—but we'll get into that another time.

We knew that we would be branded sore heads for upstaging the Russians, even though we were completely innocent. I apologized right away and explained to their officials what had happened. This incident, coupled with the pressure of the post-game press conference, couldn't have happened at a worse time.

The players were really down after the game. I wanted to go to each one, to try to console them individually, but I just didn't have the time for even a few words of encouragement. I wanted to tell them that this whole series was out of proportion anyhow; that we were just playing a hockey game and nothing more; that we weren't traitors because we spent every ounce of energy in our bodies and still couldn't carry the standard of Canada as high as we would have liked. They had to suffer alone, though, because I was at the press conference telling the world how wonderful the Russians were. This was easy, though, because they were great. They took apart the best in the world like no one ever had before.

My time together with the players came on our flight to Toronto. After we were in the air for a few minutes, I went back to their section and drew the curtain separating us from the officials up front.

"All of us lost this game tonight," I said. "Every coach and every player had a hand in it, even the ones who weren't dressed. We accept that because we're a team, and already we've been through a lot together. I don't want anyone blaming himself for what happened. When we win it will be as a team, and when we lose it's as a team. That's how it will be the whole series."

My speech was aimed toward the players who didn't do well. With seven games left to go I didn't want anyone losing his confidence.

It was a quiet ride the rest of the way. We were all tired. I ached all over as if I had played myself. My clothes were all baggy and wrinkled from perspiration. When we reached the hotel lobby all I wanted was the key to my room, a quick shower, and oblivion. As I passed through the lobby I recognized a group of people, one of whom was a pain in the ass who had talked to me before about how he could cure Bobby Orr's injured knee instantly. He supposedly healed the sore arm of John Brodie, quarterback for the San Francisco Forty-Niners.

"Harry," he said, "let me use my program on Orr and I'll have him ready to play by Thursday."

The scene was ludicrous. This was just what I needed for a nightcap. "Buddy," I told him "you take that program and jam it."

"Okay, okay," he said, knowing that I'd like to do the jamming for him.

So I sit thinking about whether I should apologize to him or not the next time I see him but not really wanting to. I've done enough apologizing today to last a lifetime.

2
Game Two

Toronto, Sept. 3

Fergie and I were both up the first thing this morning. Who could sleep much after last night? I still had that sickening feeling inside as we ordered breakfast and started to talk about the disaster of the first game. Both of us had the same thoughts. Our team became completely unglued. Instead of our style dominating, the Russian style did. Instead of making them panic and run around, we did. Instead of pressing them into mistakes, they pressed us. We realized before we finished our coffee and headed for the rink that we had to eat a little crow. We were going to have to change, not the Russians.

At Maple Leaf Gardens we studied the film of the game the night before. It didn't look any better to us. We were widely outplayed. Six times they beat us clean in one-on-one situations. You'd have to go to 20 NHL games to see a team get beaten one-on-one just twice in the same night, and here were these guys walking right by us like nothing.

It became obvious at this point that we made a mistake. We went for speed and quickness in our first lineup, yet the Russians were still faster and quicker. Now we have to slow them down. We definitely have to get our diggers into the game and try to grind the Russians down. We'll get Wayne Cashman, Jean Paul Parise and Bill Goldsworthy in there, Mikita too. And Serge Savard on defense.

The Ratelle line has to come out. It won't be effective against this team. The Ratelle line is a smooth skating and passing unit—suck a player in here, make a move there. The Russians are too fast for them, at this stage. They don't give them time to get going and they won't be sucked in. I have to get Don Awrey out of there, too. He started guessing with the Russians and committing himself first. You can't do that with these people. That's what they want—to get you running all over the place, getting out of position.

The easy part for a coach is to make the moves. The hard part is telling the players. I don't want them to be the goats. Just because they're being benched doesn't mean they blew it for us. Last night was a team effort.

With our lineup changes out of the way, we started to make a new game plan that would stop the Russian attack. They got seven goals and could have had more if they shot better and more often. We played the text book style of NHL defense against them and they tore it to pieces. The key to their success was the way their forwards could handle our defensemen in man-to-man situations in our end of the rink. We have to give our defensemen help, so I'm going to bring our forwards back deep to help out the defense. I think it will work because the Russian defensemen don't shoot well from the point. I'm trying to force the Russians to shoot from outside rather than allowing them to work the puck in deep.

In the standard NHL defensive setup, our wings would be responsible for their point men and our center would come back deep in the zone to help the defensemen. But in the first game the Russians broke out on us so quickly that our centers could never get back to help and the visitors had too many three-on-one, and two-on-one situations.

Tomorrow we'll have our center stay outside, in the middle, trying to cover their point men. Our wings will come all the way back and help in the corners. Overall, we've got to be more cautious. We made all the mistakes the first time around.

I'm not worried about our offense. We had plenty of chances last night to score more goals and just didn't shoot the puck well. Our shooting will get better as we go along. Our guys got all caught up in the excitement of the game and rushed their shots. It should be different tomorrow.

When the guys showed up for practice, I emphasized the importance of the defensive changes we were going to make. I got the feeling as I talked that the players agreed with what we were going to do. On the way out to the ice I left instructions to clear the building. I didn't want anyone to see what we were doing. This was the first time we opted for a closed practice, feeling that the players could concentrate better without any distractions.

The practice was long, but good. The players picked up the changes well and as I blew the whistle to end practice I had a good feeling. But only for a minute.

As I turned and started to skate toward the dressing room I spotted two guys sitting up back. Surer than hell—Kulagin and Bobrov. I was bullshit. They were sitting up there taking in everything we did. I was so mad I could have taken a bite right out of the boards.

Toronto, Sept. 4

The Russians couldn't have been too impressed with Kulagin and Bobrov's report on us. We put it to them tonight 4 to 1. I worried all day about the Russians adjusting to the changes we were going to make. But they didn't adjust. They just went out and played their game and I guess that's the way it's going to be for all eight of them.

We played a great game tonight. I was proud of our guys and of the fans in Maple Leaf Gardens. I never saw them so enthusiastic. This is supposed to be a staid, sophisticated, and unexcitable crowd, but tonight it was fired up. And it got to our players.

I was proud of myself and John Ferguson. I think we had as much to do with winning this game as coaches can have. All the changes we made worked. They were the difference. And our guys played a very intelligent game. We didn't run around tonight. Everything we did had a reason.

Even though we won by three goals, I'm gaining more respect for the Russians every minute. They were confused a little tonight and I had thought if we ever got them in that position, they'd panic. But they didn't. They have tremendous poise. Even when their plays weren't working they still stayed in their patterns. This is the sign of a good team. It showed me that the Russians are so well drilled that no matter what we do they won't become disorganized.

This was a helluva hockey game. Was it exciting! We've played two games in three nights and both teams have gone non-stop up and down every shift. It's like Stanley Cup . . . maybe even faster paced.

I had a good feeling about this game even before it started. I could sense that our players had respect for the Russians. They knew now that it was going to be life and death every game and that we were going to have to play steady, alert hockey to win.

The most pleasing aspect of the game for me was the way our grinders played. Parise, Cashman, Goldsworthy—these were guys picked for Team Canada because they can do a certain job. We got criticized at the time, but maybe some of the experts will think differently now. Someday they'll realize that hockey games are often won by the diggers.

We had a scoreless first period. Both teams were flying and playing well. Early in the second, we started to hit a little more and opened up the game. Cashman and Goldsworthy both took some runs at the Russians and they started to look around.

Cashman set up the first goal with his body work, getting the puck to Phil Esposito, and Phil stuffed it home.

Over two periods we outshot them 26 to 12, and near the end of the second Kharlamov drew a 10-minute misconduct. Still, after all this, we led only 1 to 0 going into the third period.

I told the guys in the dressing room before the last period they couldn't let down or start gambling. I told them if we stuck to our game plan, we'd win. And we did.

In the third period, Cournoyer broke in off the wing and put one between Tretiak's pads at 4:19. The Russians came right back with Yakushev getting sort of a cheap goal out of a scramble in front of Tony Esposito at 5:53. Then, to make it worse, Whitey Stapleton went off at 6:14 for hooking.

This looked like trouble, but Peter Mahovlich bailed us out with a great play, the best individual effort we'd had in the two games. Peter, out there as a penalty killer, got the puck and broke in on Ragulin, the Russian defenseman. Pete put him to the ice with a fake slap shot, and then went around him and in on Tretiak to score with another nice move. Finally, we beat them in a man-to-man situation. This was a blow to the Russians, and when Frank Mahovlich scored on a shot off the pipe two minutes later, it was as good as over. Boy, were our players happy! We weren't traitors any more.

It was my first coaching victory—in a genuine game—since the day we won the Stanley Cup in Boston. Right now I can't honestly say which felt better. But this one sure felt good.

3
Game Three

Winnipeg, Sept. 5th

This wasn't one of my better days. I guess one thing about coaching is that you never get to savor anything very long. There's always another day and the possibility of the anguish of losing. I usually look at it the other way, on the positive side, the exhilaration of winning. But I didn't find very much positive in my thoughts in the past twelve hours.

This morning, before we left Toronto on our flight here, I had the first real player problem since we got the team together three weeks ago. Vic Hadfield threatened to quit. I guess his ego's bruised because I sat him down in Toronto last night. The fact that we won doesn't seem to matter.

Hadfield asked me, "What's going on? Am I going to play or aren't I? If I'm not, I'm going home. I'm not going out West to sit around."

I told Vic I couldn't guarantee him or anyone else that they'd be in the lineup. Hell, this team is going to be what John Ferguson and I want it to be, not what Vic Hadfield or any other player wants.

We took different planes here today, and I didn't know if

Hadfield stayed at home or not until we got here and I saw him. I know other members of the team are mumbling about not playing. Hadfield's the only one who came to me, but I can sense the same feeling in some of the others. I asked Rod Gilbert about it, feeling that he might be shook up too, because Ratelle played and he and Vic didn't. "Listen coach," Rod told me, "do what you think is best. You're the coach and I'll go along with it."

Then I had a little session with Mr. Clarence Campbell. Saturday night, after we were beaten 7 to 3, he put the knock on me and some of my players pretty good. I was incensed when I found out about it Monday when the story came out in the paper. Basically, Campbell claimed I didn't play the right men—that I tried to appease the people in Montreal by starting Ken Dryden in goal and Guy LaPointe on defense. He also got in a few more digs.

The whole thing was really bush league. Can you imagine a guy of Campbell's stature doing something like that? Here's a guy putting down some of the best players in the league—his league—because of one game. Dryden was so upset about it he went to see Campbell personally to tell him what he thought.

Naturally, the writers tried to get me to fire back at Campbell but I didn't. What really stunned me was that he had been in our corner all the way. He's been behind almost everything we'd tried to do with Team Canada.

In the course of his conversation with Campbell, Dryden told him that I was burning. When I got to the hotel today I had a call from the NHL president. "I understand you're mad at me," he said. I told him how I felt. He said that he was only giving a 'post mortem' on the game and that what he said didn't come out in print the way he intended.

I told him: "Listen, you don't have any control over me or Team Canada. So to me you're just another fan. If you want to get carried away and be critical of us over one loss, that's your right as a fan."

To tell the truth, if I had been coaching the Bruins, or any team in the NHL for that matter, and Campbell pulled the same thing, I'd have gone after him like no one ever went after him before. But in this situation, he was just another fan.

I'm just placing Campbell in the same group as those other 'loyal' Canadians I heard from after the Montreal opener. I got over a hundred telegrams the next couple of days and with the exception of one, they put the hammer to the team. The good one came from the U.S. and my pal Tom Johnson, coach of the Bruins. "Keep playing your own game and you'll be okay," Tom wired. I got some encouragement over the phone from class guys like Tommy Ivan and Sam Pollack, too. The fans weren't nice though. The wires were mostly garbage like "Way to go, Harry. Keep up the good work." Or, "Will be in town tomorrow to inspect some of your clowns for our new circus. Signed, Barnum and Bailey." I didn't read all of them. Bobby Haggert did and he said they were very nasty.

As I sit here thinking about all this, I just can't figure it out. Wasn't it just a hockey game? Or was it a World War or something? Couldn't the fans just accept the fact that we lost to a helluva hockey team and let it go at that? They couldn't say the players didn't put out. They gave as much as any team I've ever seen in the NHL give in a single game.

Now that we have beaten the Russians, I wonder if Bobrov is getting hate mail from Russia. Who knows, maybe the Soviet Minister of Sport put the zing to him in Izvestia for playing the wrong lineup.

Winnipeg, Sept. 6th

We had another great hockey game tonight. We didn't win, but it was still a great game. I told the writers after the game, "Aren't we all glad to be alive and watching this kind of hockey?" Someone once said that a tie is as exciting as kissing your sister. Well for the last 10 minutes tonight that hockey game—4 to 4—looked like Racquel Welch to me.

It was a strange game. At one point in the second period I thought we were going to run away from them. That was after Paul Henderson's goal put us ahead 4 to 2 at 13:47. Until that time we had it all over them. Our players were operating the same way we did in Toronto. The first two Russian goals came from our mistakes while they were shorthanded. Outside of a couple of bad plays that allowed them to cash in, we had it going good.

J.P. Parise, the guy that wasn't good enough to make this team according to some people, scored our first goal with a real digging effort. Petrov tied it up for them at 3:16 of the first when Frank Mahovlich made a bad pass while we were on the power play. Petrov grabbed it at our blue line and moved in to beat Tony Esposito between the pads. Tony played the angle well but the Russian just found the crack in his pads and hit the spot.

Near the end of the period Ratelle put us back in front 2 to 1. Then at the start of the final period Phil Esposito got our third goal and I felt we had their number. Phil had been our best player. What a competitor! At times in training camp I wondered how he was going to play without Bobby Orr on the team. Those two complement each other so beautifully that I felt Phil might not be the same super player without Orr. But he's shown me and anyone else who might have had the same doubt. The guy has been a super competitor. He just keeps going no matter what the situation is.

The Russians got their second goal at 12:56, again while they were shorthanded. Our guys just didn't think. We know what the Russians do when they've got a man in the penalty box. When they're in their own end, and one of their forwards gets the puck, the other forward just takes off up ice and the guy with the puck tries to bounce it off the boards to him looking for the quick break. We've warned our guys about this but we're still getting burned.

Again Henderson put us back in front 4 to 2 less than a minute after the Russian goal and I figured there wasn't any way they were going to catch us. I was wrong. Before you could pronounce most of their names they were back with two goals in the last five minutes of the period to tie it up. We had outshot them 32 to 17, in two periods, yet we were fighting to hold on.

That's what we did in the third period—hold on. For the first time in the series their superior conditioning did us in. In the final 10 minutes of the game our guys were gone physically. They just didn't have anything left to give. I thought for sure the Russians were going to beat us near the end. They could have. They had chances and let them get away. If they had shot more when they had the opportunities they could have won. Geez, I'm glad they didn't.

I have to give the Russians all the credit in the world. When we were ahead 4 to 2, and playing so well, I thought we were getting ready for a romp. But they didn't lose their poise, and they got those two goals back so easily I was really shook up. When they tied it up I went running down the bench and yelled to Fergie: "What the hell is going on here? They're all

The Canadian team and officials pose at a practice session in Maple Leaf Gardens. (Photo by the Toronto Star)

Things looked good when Bobby Orr was able to join the squad's skating sessions—but that knee wasn't ready. (Photo by C.P.)

Harry Sinden organising the Canadian team at a Toronto practice session.
(Photo by C.P.)

The Assistant Coach of the Russian Team, Boris Kulagin, puts his players
through their paces in Montreal. (Photo La Presse)

Game One, Montreal, September 2. Prime Minister Pierre Trudeau drops the puck while Esposito faces off against Vikulov. Russian Coach Bobrov and Canadian Assistant Coach John Ferguson appear at the back of the official party. (Photo by C.P.)

All eyes are on the puck as it flies in front of Tsigankov, with Henderson and Ellis ready to pounce. (Photo by C.P.)

In the Montreal game Kharlamov scored two second period goals to set the Russians on the way to their stunning 7 - 3 win. (Photo by the Montreal Gazette)

There were no arguments when Kharlamov was named the game's Most Valuable Player. (Photo by C.P.)

Game Two, Toronto, September 4. Mishakov makes a move to go around Bergman and Park in the first period. (Photo by C.P.)

Yvan Cournoyer speeds in and fires the puck between Tretiak's legs for the decisive goal. (Photo by C.P.)

Peter Mahovlich's unforgettable clinching goal, scored with Pat Stapleton in the penalty box. Mahovlich's great individual effort left him draped over the goal and the beaten Tretiak. (Photo by C.P.)

Game Three, Winnipeg, September 6. Wayne Cashman and Yuri Shatalov
crunch together. (Photo by C.P.)

Game Four, Vancouver, September 8. With Goldsworthy in the penalty box, Boris Mikhailov tips in one of his two first period goals. Dryden vainly slides across while Bill White can only watch in horror. (Photo by the Vancouver Province).

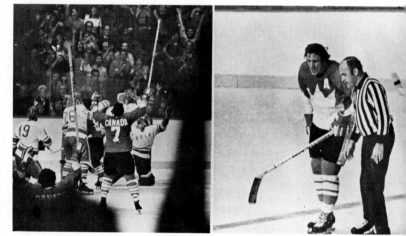

Jubilation as Rod Gilbert scores a vital goal for the trailing Canadian team—only for the goal to be disallowed, despite Phil Esposito's protests. (Photo by C.P.)

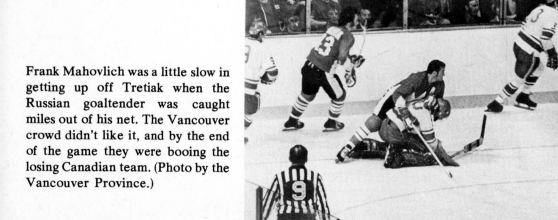

Frank Mahovlich was a little slow in getting up off Tretiak when the Russian goaltender was caught miles out of his net. The Vancouver crowd didn't like it, and by the end of the game they were booing the losing Canadian team. (Photo by the Vancouver Province.)

over the place. Are they putting eight guys out there or something? Why the hell is this happening to me? I'm just a little guy from Rochester."

Fergie didn't know exactly what to make of me. "I know how you feel," he said. "I know just how you feel." We felt like Butch Cassidy and the Sundance Kid in the final scene of the movie. They were down in South America robbing banks when the local army finally caught up with them and had them pinned down in a shack, coming at them from all over the place, trying to shoot their butts off. Finally, Butch says to Sundance: "Who are those guys?"

Here were these guys who all look the same, skate the same, shoot the same, the whole game without ever changing expression. They just keep coming after you and the only thing different about them is the number on their backs. I've never had to contend with anything like this in my life before!

4
Game Four

Vancouver, Sept. 7th

After reviewing the films of our game in Winnipeg our feelings were confirmed. We ran out of gas near the end. Three games in five days were too much for some of our guys to handle at this stage in the season. The games had all the fury and heavy skating of Stanley Cup play, only our players didn't have 85 games to build themselves up to that kind of pace.

So we're going to change our lineup for the game here tomorrow night. In the last two games, the team that came on with fresh legs had the best of it. In Toronto we used five new men. In Winnipeg, the Russians made five changes and their new faces played extremely well.

Coming into the series our goaltending plan was to start Dryden in the first game, Esposito in the second, come back in the third with whoever played the best goal in those two games, then have Eddie Johnston finish up in Vancouver. But the first game of the series changed all that. When we made those plans we never expected to be coming here with just one win. We have to go all out in this one so we can at least go to Russia for the final four games with some kind of edge.

Tony Esposito played well in the second and third games. He's faced a lot of pressure for this stage of the season so we're leaning toward Dryden. In the past couple of years these two guys have been fighting each other to be the best goalie in hockey. I believe the experts consider them 1-2, take your pick, in the NHL.

Just for the record, we opened the series with Dryden in Montreal because, regardless of the outcome, Ken and Tony were going to split the first two games. Secondly, it was Dryden's home rink and it is an advantage to any player, whether he's on a golf course, tennis court, or football field, to be playing on familiar turf.

Every rink is different, and Ken Dryden has had a pretty fair record in the Forum. Now we're coming back with Dryden on a hunch. Fergie thinks the guy is a helluva competitor, and so do I. We both thought that he might have felt upstaged by Tony's work in the last couple of games and would be chomping at the bit to get back at the Russians.

We'll make some other changes, but the only one I'm sure of right now is Gilles Perreault. He hasn't played yet in this series, but maybe it's time to give him a shot. The kid's a great player and maybe he can give us some kind of spark. I might get Gilbert and Hadfield back into the lineup, but not with Ratelle. They've both had five days to rest so we should be able to get a strong 60 minutes out of them.

I am concerned about the officiating as much as I am about our stamina. The referees folded a little bit in the third game. After we beat them in Toronto, the Russians beefed in the newspapers about the officiating. And referees read the papers. So they were on Cashman's back all night in Winnipeg. As Phil Esposito said later: "I've seen Cash tailed by cops, but never by a referee before. They were right with him all night." I'm afraid now he's a marked man. We'll probably have the same refs back tomorrow night so I'll get Cash to sit it out.

I realize more than ever now—especially after a deal like that with Cashman in Winnipeg—that we should have made them play NHL rules with NHL officials. They have the biggest advantage of all playing us this time of year, which is the worst time for us. If we had to give away the dates in their favor, then we should have at least been allowed our own rules. But the people who made the deal felt we'd beat this team in a breeze under any rules.

They know differently now.

Vancouver, Sept. 8th

I've been so involved with these Russians the last couple of months I must be starting to talk like them. Before tonight's game I took Bill Goldsworthy aside and told him I wanted to make up for some of the muscle we're losing with Cashman sitting in the stands tonight. "Now listen," I said "I don't want you going out of your way to take a cheap shot at these guys. Just make sure that every time you go into the corner with one of them that you come out with the final word. Get that last lick in so that they'll know we're around."

So what does Goldy do? His first shift he goes right over our boards to cross-check a guy, and gets a penalty. After he serves the penalty he comes back to our bench and I say to him, "What are you doing? That thing was a penalty all the way. I didn't tell you to do that. Let's wake up out there."

"Okay, Harry. Don't worry," he says.

Don't worry? Two minutes later he's back in the box after trying to fracture one of them with his elbow. The Russians score a power play goal each time he's off and we're down 2 to 0 in the first seven minutes on the way to a 5 to 3 beating. But then I shouldn't blame Goldy. He does what he's told, and I told him to do it.

And that's what it was, a beating. The score was a lot closer than the game. We were never in it. We mustn't have even warmed up well because, for some reason, the Vancouver fans started booing us before the game even started. And they didn't let up the rest of the way, either. We didn't give them any reason to, though, because we put together a terrible performance. We just didn't have a thing, and this game was very dull compared to the others.

It was our fault, not the Russians'. We couldn't even make a good game out of it tonight. They're really amazing. I have seen them play four games now, and they've played every one at the same pace. They don't have ups and downs. Everything is consistent. Their teamwork is truly amazing.

Right now they're as good as any team in the world. I'm not saying they'd win the Stanley Cup, but I am saying that if the Russians were in the NHL this 1972-73 season, they would have to be rated with Boston and New York as the favorites.

Looking back at this game, I can see I made a mistake by changing our lineup. We should have stuck with the guys who won for us in Toronto. That's our best lineup. We started Dryden and he didn't have a good game. He was very shaky. I've never seen him have as hard a time with relatively easy shots as he did tonight. But the funny thing is that all our goals came from the new guys. Perreault got one for us with a great individual effort. Dennis Hull and Goldsworthy got the others.

Tretiak is great. He's giving our players real trouble. We thought he wouldn't be very good on high shots, and his glove hand was suspect. Neither turned out to be a weakness. The kid is one helluva goaltender and the pressure isn't bothering him. In every game we could have scored four or five more goals, but either he made a great play, or our guys just didn't click around the net. So far, we haven't been good around the net.

The only real weakness I can see right now in the Russians is that they aren't terribly good in their own end. They give away too many good shots. What saves them many times is their goalie and the way they break out of their end. Once they get the puck, the chase is on.

With them, every trip up ice is a threat, which isn't so with NHL teams. The Russians seem to get a good chance on goal almost every time they handle the puck. In the NHL this happens only about every four times. The difference is in the way the Russians handle the puck and work for the good shot. We've been outshooting them in this series, but most of our shots are coming from downtown. Their shots are from right in front and from good angles. Tonight they also showed us they could do some of "our own" things well. Their first two goals were tip-ins by Mikhailov. "That's the old Canadiens style," Fergie said later.

Once again the officiating hurt us. When we were behind 3 to 1 in the second, Gilbert scored a goal. The referee blew it and wouldn't allow it. He said that Gilbert kicked it in, which is illegal. But Gilbert didn't kick it in. Hadfield slid a pass across in front and the puck bounced in off Gilbert's skates. To me that was the turning point of the game. If that goal had been allowed it could have been a different game.

But it wasn't our night anyway. It's a shame to close out the Canadian part of the series playing so poorly. Now the Russians are going home in great shape pyschologically. They came to Canada saying their goal was to "learn something from these great professionals." Leaving Canada, Coach Kulagin's line was slightly different: "We never expected such a result here. The Canadians are the equal of the Soviet team."

I'm glad he feels that way, because at this moment I'm not sure I do.

Interim

I'm home on a little vacation between the finish of our series in Canada and the start of our trip to Europe. In trying to relax a bit, and to stop my mind from constantly whirling with thoughts about the series, my wife and I went out with some neighbors for dinner and a few drinks last night. This is the kind of series you can't escape, I guess, because pretty soon we were back to hockey. I must have been feeling sorry for myself. "How did you ever get yourself into this?" is a question that flashed through my mind several times. I realize now that 40 years of crazy bounces directed me to this improbable position.

Three different times in my career I walked away from professional hockey, the last being when I quit as coach of the Boston Bruins after we won the Stanley Cup 2½ years ago. At that time I said I had never wanted to be in hockey all my life, that I had wanted other things. I felt I wasn't my own man at times, and many years ago I had decided never to get caught in that rut.

What I didn't count on when I walked out of Boston was

37

missing the game. I had never been away from it before in my life, and I didn't know I would miss it as much as I did. Even though I was working in the home building industry in Rochester with the Stirling Homex Company and was completely divorced from the game, I found myself listening to hockey games at night from Boston, Buffalo, or Toronto. And whenever I was in any of these cities, and there was a game, I'd always be at it. As I sit here in my back yard making this tape, the sun shining on my face on a bright September afternoon, I have come to believe that hockey never leaves the blood of a Canadian. You like to think you're more mature than that, that a game shouldn't mean that much, but it does.

Why else would the people react the way they did to the Russians beating us last week? Their pride was hurt. This is the Canadian game and now someone is trying to take it away from us. To a non-Canadian this might seem absurd, but in Canada, hockey is *the* game. Everyone plays it, and their fathers and grandfathers played it before them. It is a Canadian tradition to want to be good enough to play in the National Hockey League. I wasn't any different, but I never thought it would lead to something like this, general manager and head coach of Team Canada. I never envisioned myself making tapes, keeping notes, and saving clips to write a book about this series.

I look back on my life as perhaps typical of Canadians born in my generation. I was born of immigrant parents in Toronto in 1932, their second child. (My sister Betty is a year older.) My mother came to Canada from Scotland when she was 18. My father came over from England when he was just a year old, so he was a Canadian.

My dad was a gentleman and a gentle man. Any athletic ability I had must have come from him. He was a fine athlete, playing almost all sports well and reaching Senior Amateur status as a hockey player. It was my dad—Harry J. Sinden Sr.—who wanted me to be a hockey player. Yet he never pushed me, and I will always be grateful for that. I read and hear nowadays about parents who shove their kids into sports, and it only makes my love for my father that much greater. He died in 1964 and one of my greatest regrets is that he wasn't alive to see me coach a Stanley Cup winner, or that he wasn't here this year when I was accorded the honor of being selected coach of Team Canada. He would have been the proudest father alive.

We didn't have money when I was growing up. I'd describe our social status as lower-middle class. Our first home was with my grandparents on Marchmount Road in Toronto. I don't remember very much about the house, though, because when I was five we moved outside of Toronto to a small section called York Township.

This was the start of my romance with hockey. Across the street from our house were two large hockey cushions—that's what we called them—outdoor natural ice surfaces surrounded by boards. For the next 10 years those cushions were, in reality, my home. Every free moment I had was spent playing hockey or just skating. At the same time, through the fantasy made possible by radio, I became a Toronto Maple Leaf nut. I can vividly recall lying in bed listening to Foster Hewitt broadcast the Leafs' game, and crying my eyes out if they lost. And I mean cry.

Of course, my father nurtured this budding love of the sport. When I was six, he bought me a Toronto Maple Leafs sweater and stockings for Christmas. They became my most prized possessions. I got my first pair of skates about the same time, but even before I used to go out to my back yard and "skate" on my shoes. There was a big puddle in the yard that froze over in winter, and on it each afternoon was Harry J. Sinden Jr., steam curling up from his mouth, announcing the game as he played it. "Apps has the puck . . . He passes to Drillon . . . There's a shot . . . Maple Leafs goal!" Those were wonderful moments for me. I was completely wrapped up in hockey.

My first pair of skates were Bob skates, the double runners you strapped onto your shoes. Saturdays I would go over to the cushions in the morning; come home for lunch and eat with my skates on; go back and play hockey; and return when my mother put the light on upstairs, my signal to come home.

My dad was very busy in those days. We never spent the time together a father and his young son should have, especially since we were so much alike. It was during the depression and he was working three jobs. His main job was as building superintendent for the Ontario Hydro Electric Power Commission, but he was also a janitor at a school, and he spray painted cars on weekends. He worked four to midnight and we mostly just saw each other coming and going.

As I grew up, I started in other sports. I played softball, ran the half mile for the high school track team, and was a good basketball player. My specialty was the two-handed set shot, which eventually went the way of double-runner skates. I knew, though, that if I was ever going anywhere as an athlete, it would be in hockey.

I was handicapped in the game at this time because York was a small town and didn't have any organized hockey. To me hockey was going to one of the cushions at eight in the morning and playing with three or four other kids until ten. By this time, there would be 150 kids skating in all directions with 15 games going at once. I got a pair of gloves to go with my sweater and stockings, and my first pair of shin pads were rolled-up magazines taped under my stockings. By the end of winter, I had played so much with my stick that the blade was worn as thin as a toothpick.

Organized hockey began for me at 14, which is late. Some kids from the community were playing on a team in Toronto, and one day they asked me to go with them.

I found out why they asked me—they didn't have anyone who could play the game at all. We got skunked 15 to 1, and yours truly got the only goal for our side. I was so thrilled I could have walked all the way home. But I took the street car and my dad was waiting for me when I got off. When I told him I got a goal his face lit up. I forgot to tell him the score.

In those days, there weren't as many organized hockey programs for kids as there are today. Kids didn't really start playing until they were 13, and most of the high schools, like mine, didn't have hockey teams. (I did well in school—in the top five percent of my class—at least partly because I didn't have hockey to distract me.)

The door to better hockey—and the end to family life as a kid should know it—opened when I was 16. The previous year, a scout for the Montreal Canadiens watched me in a midget game and lined me up for training camp the next season. They took just five midget-aged boys from Ontario to Montreal for the tryouts, so I was very proud. I had never been outside of Ontario before, so the train ride to Montreal was extra special for a kid who now envisioned himself well on the way to a Hall of Fame career.

The tryout was in September, 1948. The Canadiens had four teams working out every day in the Forum—the Montreal Junior Canadiens, the Montreal Junior Royals, the Montreal Nationals and the Verdun Maple Leafs. I was assigned to

Verdun, and, to be honest, played quite well in that camp. I wish I could remember all the kids who were there because a bunch of them went on to become stars. I remember Dickie Moore and Boom Boom Geoffrion for sure.

I did well enough in the workouts for the Canadiens to ask me to sign to play junior hockey in Oshawa, Ontario. This was fine with me, because I wanted in the worst way to play in the NHL and Oshawa was a good place to start—just 35 miles from my home.

In Oshawa, where somebody named Bobby Orr would get his start two decades later, the Harry J. Sinden express became a freight train. I spent four years in Oshawa, none of them noteworthy. Our team was poor, and I think this might have hurt my chances, even though individually I did fairly well. General Motors had sponsored a team in prior years, and despite dropping its sponsorship, gave players jobs and saw to it that they had to work only half a shift the day of a game.

So in my last years as a junior—I was 20—I had to make the toughest decision of my life. I was getting married, but I was also asked to attend the Boston Bruins training camp in Hershey, Pennsylvania. I gave it a lot of thought, but in the end decided I wasn't good enough. I had a job with General Motors in Oshawa as a stationary engineer in a power house. The power house was powerful security to me. The NHL, though it offered glamor, seemed beyond my reach. Besides, I rationalized, I had a chance right in Oshawa to play a caliber of hockey that was as good as any minor league brand—Senior Amateur hockey for the Whitby-Dunlops.

To me, this was a great way to live. I was making $60 a week as an engineer and $15 per game as a hockey player. We played a 54 game schedule in an 8 team league. I was a defenseman, but I wasn't rough. I could handle the puck well and get plays moving. I was more offensive than defensive. Even as a kid, I understood that sound offensive movement, whether it was in hockey, basketball, soccer or whatever, depends upon getting open to take a pass, and upon hitting the open man with a pass. As a skater, I was strong but not quick. The biggest detriment to my chances of getting to the NHL was my skating.

I had had a good time when playing in Oshawa as a junior. We—three other players and I—lived in Mrs. Hastings' boarding house and enjoyed being teenagers on our own. I met my wife in Oshawa on a blind date. She was supposed to go out with one of my buddies, and when he couldn't make it I stepped in. That was one time I didn't mind being a substitute.

After our marriage, I became just Joe ordinary Jock, working for General Motors during the day, playing senior hockey at night. Our team practiced every night. Over the next five years we would win a Provincial championship, two National championships, and one World championship. We had some great players, guys who definitely would have played in the National Hockey League if it hadn't been such a clique—just six teams—in those days. To be perfectly honest, I never considered myself an NHL player until I got up to the league and started coaching. Then I realized that perhaps myself, and a lot of other guys like me, could have made it.

It was just about this time (the early 50s) that the rivalry between Canada and Russia started. Prior to this, the World Championship was a joke. In 1948, the Canadian team had won a game in the World Cup playoffs 47 to 0. It sounds impossible but it happened. Then in 1954 the Russians, making their first appearance in International hockey, floored the Canadian nation by beating our team 7 to 2.

Reading about it then got me stirred up. I can remember the guys on our team talking about getting a shot at the Russians. We felt that the team which lost to the USSR, sponsored by a Toronto car dealer, was not a good one.

Our team wouldn't get first crack at the Russians. A team from British Columbia, featuring the fabled Warwick brothers, crushed the Soviets 5 to 0 the following year and salvaged our pride. But not for long. In 1956, Russia beat Canada in the Olympic final, and now the nation was incensed. Because of this, it was decided that the senior team which won the national championship one year would represent the country in international play the next.

In 1957, we won the National title—the Allen Cup. Now I had another big decision to make. Cleveland, in the American Hockey League, offered me a pro contract. It was a two-year deal calling for a $2000 bonus and $4500 each season. I had been waiting for something like this for years, but in the end I declined. It may sound corny, but I wanted to play for my country in the World Championships in 1958.

The Russians had made their first visit to North America in 1957, swinging through Canada to play a series of games. This is when I played against them for the first time. Our Whitby-Dunlop team, in front of one of the largest crowds ever to see a game in Maple Leaf Gardens to that time, beat the Russians 7 to 2. They scored both goals in the first minute, before we ran all over them. They weren't that bad, though. Before they left, they whipped a collection of Canada's best junior all-stars 10 to 0. On that team were future NHL greats Bob Nevin, Bob Pulford, Ralph Backstrom.

We kept that beating in mind the next year as we left for Oslo to get the World Championship back for Canada. I had never been out of the country before and my first trip abroad was one I'd just as soon forget.

Wren Blair, our coach, decided he didn't want us to fly. So we went by boat. I didn't think this was the best way to get a hockey team ready for a tournament—ten days in the rough North Atlantic in the middle of winter.

The ocean voyage didn't bother us once we hit land, though. We moved into the finals against Russia with little difficulty. The final, played on a Sunday afternoon, was a great scene—a huge outdoor stadium filled with 18,000 shivering people. As we drove up in a school bus—we had to dress about five miles from the rink—I remember thinking about the telegram we had received from Prime Minister Diefenbaker and signed by thousands of Canadians, urging us to win.

We were too excited and started slowly. We froze up, and not from the weather. But we caught them with a pair of goals near the end of the third period to beat them 4 to 2.

As best as I can remember, the Russians didn't skate or shoot then as well as they do now. In those days, they would never take a bad shot and virtually all their plays started in the corner. Then they would concentrate on getting the puck into an area about 20 feet directly in front of the goalie before shooting. When we finally broke that pattern, we beat them and I had the chance to get my picture taken on the podium.

I'll tell you one thing: I didn't feel like Charley Chaplin when I was accepting the World Cup. I felt more like King Kong.

Rochester, Sept. 12

When things go bad, it never seems to end.

I was sitting at home with my trusty tape recorder when the phone rang.

"Harry, this is Al Eagleson. We've got a problem."

"What's that, Al?"

"Frank Mahovlich. His doctor doesn't want him to take the trip to Europe. Says Frank is too keyed up about this thing and needs a rest."

"You're kidding."

"I'm not. I talked to the doctors this morning and they don't want to let him go under any circumstances. He's really uptight about this thing and they're afraid the trip wouldn't help him at all."

To tell the truth, I wasn't surprised. Big Frank took this series personally. And when we lost those games to the Russians he was really distraught. After one of them he came up to me and said, "Harry, if you brought a football to Russia, in two years those guys would be back to win the Super Bowl."

I had never coached Frank before, or spent that much time around him, so I thought this was just his way. I knew he was a very serious guy who was churning inside all the time. So when I saw him worrying about little things that wouldn't bother most guys I thought it was just his way.

When I played back the tape I made yesterday I thought, "that's too corny" when I went over the part about hockey being in a Canadian's blood. Well, this thing with Frank couldn't prove my point better. It really hurts when you lose for your country, more so than if you lose just as an individual, or as a team. Playing for your nation involves some kinds of special emotions. Just look at the way those kids in the Olympics cry over winning and losing.

I experienced those emotions in 1960, when I was part of an excellent team that deserved to win the Olympics in Squaw Valley, California, and didn't. Our team played 31 games that year and lost just once, to the United States, 2 to 1. We took 50 shots to their 17, but unbelievable goaltending by Jack McCartan beat us. We clobbered the Russians 9 to 3 in the games which ultimately gave the United States the Gold Medal. Losing that Gold was the most disappointing thing in my hockey career. It stayed with me a long time.

I didn't know it at the time, but after the Olympics my amateur career was coming to a close. Shortly after I arrived back home in Oshawa, Sam Pollack called and asked to me play for the Hull-Ottawa Canadiens in the Eastern Professional Hockey League. Sam, now general manager of the Montreal

Canadiens, was running Hull-Ottawa then and wanted me for the playoffs. He explained to me that the rules stated an amateur could play eight games for a professional team before losing his amateur status.

When I started travelling back and forth to play for Pollack's team, I kept on bumping into Lynn Patrick, then general manager of the Boston Bruins. Lynn was following the series as a scout, and it so happened we wound up on a lot of the same planes and trains during the series, always talking hockey.

This new relationship didn't have any significance until the following summer when Lynn appointed Wren Blair coach of Kingston, the Bruins' affiliate in the Eastern Pro League. At the same time, Patrick asked Blair if I would be interested in coaching the Bruins' junior team in Oshawa. Blair said sure, but, instead, when he came to me he offered me a job as player-assistant coach with his Kingston club. So, after all those years with General Motors, the hockey corpuscles in my blood got the best of me. At 28, I was giving up my seniority, my security and all my experience in my job for the same money I made at General Motors.

I was apprehensive, but I finally talked myself into it by saying I'd make the same money in six months playing hockey that it took a year to make at the plant. Besides,the chance to coach intrigued me; my thoughts always had been just about playing. I was player-coach in Kingston for two years and we won a championship one of those seasons. Then we moved the franchise to Minneapolis for two years, and then down to Oklahoma City. It was my fifth year of coaching and by far my most interesting.

We took hockey into Oklahoma City for the first time and no one there knew a thing about the game. We had to give clinics for the fans so they'd understand the rules, and what the game was supposed to be all about.

You know something, by Christmas, those people sitting up in the stands with their cowboy hats on were 'experts'. We played some of the most unusual games you'd ever want to witness in Oke City that year. The ice at the Arena was very temporary and they used plastic pipes underneath. The resulting ice surface was rubbery at times, and wavy. We must have adjusted to it because we won the championship and had one of the most successful minor league franchises in the business that season.

So it wasn't totally unfounded when I started getting the feeling I might be on my way up to the Bruins. No one said anything to me at this point, but I knew Milt Schmidt was being moved upstairs and that his coaching job would be open.

Silly as it seems, part of me didn't want that job. I had a chip on my shoulder against the National Hockey League. I thought I should have been playing in it a few years earlier. When I was with Kingston I was leading all defensemen in scoring, and winning the league's Most Valuable Player award. This didn't seem to impress the Bruins. Cellar Dwellers every year, they kept taking guys up from our Kingston team who I knew weren't any better than I was. But I was dumb. I should have spoken up. In those days no one talked back. You got up in the morning, did your job, and kept your mouth shut. It's ridiculous that I never got a chance and I will always be bitter about that.

Lynn Patrick actually got me the job. He was in the process of being fired as general manager. Schmidt was being moved upstairs to the front office, and Hap Emms, who had run the Bruins junior team in Niagara Falls, was general manager. Before he left, Patrick told Weston Adams Sr., president of the Bruins, that I was ready to coach in the NHL. So Adams sent Emms down to sign me. I signed a two-year contract at $15,000 per year, which was stupid. Every coach in the NHL was making over $20,000 at the time, but I was so anxious for the job I jumped at the 15 G's. I had made $10,000 coaching at Oklahoma City, so I thought it was a big raise.

To show you how ridiculous that figure is by comparison, I talked with Derek Sanderson after one of the games in this series and he told me he is going to be paid $400,000 this year alone for playing with the Philadelphia team in the new World Hockey Association. And part of his $2.6 million deal gives Derek's father a full-time job as a scout for Philadelphia, making more money scouting than I ever made coaching the Bruins, even when we won the Stanley Cup.

Like I said before, the money didn't bother me at the time because I didn't know any better. To me the drawback was not being able to play any more. I was 33 years old and I wanted to play in the NHL. But I kept my mouth shut and went along.

Somewhere over the Atlantic Sept. 13

If someone could grant me a wish right now, I'd wish I could go back to the day I decided to pick a 35-man squad for Team Canada—and then I'd punch myself in the head for getting such a stupid thought. I wonder now, if we should have picked a smaller team to work with.

We've been up in the air a few hours now on the long trip to Europe, and my mind keeps telling me we'd have a much better chance in our remaining games if we could settle on a set lineup. Even though it might hurt some of the other guys' feelings, when we get to Sweden I'm going to concentrate on the guys who will be playing in Russia, basically the guys who won for us in Toronto last week.

I know the players who are being pushed aside aren't going to like it. I can still sense a feeling of unhappiness among some of the guys who haven't played much, but I can't let that interfere with my decisions. They knew what the deal was when they signed on, and the rules haven't changed. One of the first things I learned when I started coaching NHL players is that they tend to get priorities confused. When I first took over the Bruins, a last place team for years, I had a group of guys who wanted glory and fame, without earning it. They wanted it regardless of how they played the game, and that's impossible. All the benefits come only from winning. The game isn't fun unless you win. The Bruins had been losing for so long, they really didn't know what it was to win. Most of them thought that just playing in the NHL would set up all the other rewards for them.

I handled that situation the best way I thought possible—we got rid of most of them as quickly as we could. You keep losers around long enough and they'll pull the winners right down with them.

My lessons from the Bruins are becoming invaluable in this experience. My first year as coach of the Bruins I insisted I would run practices and games my way, and use players as I saw fit. Hap Emms was the general manager and he pretty much decided who would stay or go. Emms never liked the way I did things. He wanted to run the show himself. He wanted to come on the ice when I was coaching; he wanted to come into the locker room during and after games to address the team; and he was always finding fault with the way I did things. I really resented it at the time. He was using me as a crutch for the problems of the organization.

When I talked with the officials of Hockey Canada about this team I kept Hap in mind. I insisted I would run the show and call all the shots without any interference. I'm glad now that I did, because if it had been otherwise, I'm sure I'd have 15 guys wanting to do my job for me. A sound organization can't operate that way. If you hire a guy to do a job you have to let him do it his way. If it isn't good enough, then get someone else who can do the job.

That's what ruined the Boston organization for me when I was coaching there. The front office was always second guessing me and the players. My first year coaching the Bruins was very tough. I worked harder at coaching that year than I ever did in my life. I put all kinds of hours into the job, working with players individually on the ice and having meeting after meeting in order to improve the club. Still, we didn't seem to be getting any better. This made me an easy target for the front office. "He has never played in the league," was one routine. The other was I was too young. I took the team all the way from fifth to sixth that year. We ended in great fashion. During the closing moments of our final game in Boston Gardens, the pipes under the ice burst and started shooting water straight up in the air.

The only thing that saved my sanity was watching Bobby Orr play. He was a rookie, injured a lot, and somewhat frustrated by the ineptness of our team. Orr had problems that year because he was trying to do it all alone. We just didn't have any help for him. Most of our guys up front were little— Pat Martin, Murray Oliver, Ron Shock, Wayne Connelly. You could get away with that if you played the game like the Russians. But in the NHL style of shooting the puck into the corners and pounding in after it, you have to have the people who are going to come out of the corner with the puck most of the time.

Hap Emms departed Boston at the end of the season and Milt Schmidt moved up to become general manager. My second year as coach was a different story. We went out and got some new people and made the great trade with Chicago that brought Esposito, Ken Hodge, and Fred Stanfield to Boston. We also had Sanderson coming up to be Rookie of the Year, and Ted Green came back well after knee surgery.

Suddenly, the midgets were gone and we had a big, potentially physical team. And this is what we decided to be.

Everyone else in the league but us had an identity or an image. Chicago could shoot. New York could pass. Montreal could skate. Detroit could forecheck. Toronto had back-checking. Boston had nothing. We changed that in quick order. We began letting the rest of the league know what was in store for them when they played us. We let them know that if they wanted to beat us they were going to take their lumps to do it.

Playing this way we finished third, setting up a meeting with Montreal in the playoffs. They toyed with us, knocking us off in four quick games. We never could intimidate them in that series because John Ferguson kept fighting all their battles for them. We thought we could get to some of their little forwards and beat hell out of them, but Fergie became the equalizer. Montreal was the better team, and when they breezed through three Stanley Cup playoff series that year, they left little doubt about it.

I was still pleased with our season. It showed me that we were headed in the right direction. We fostered the image of the big, bad Bruins and nurtured it every way we could. It was helping us win. We were intimidating teams. Our reputation was spreading and helping us to win games, because some teams were not prepared to play this style.

The irony is that, deep down, I think hockey and fighting shouldn't go together. Fighting is a part of pro hockey and sadly so. There are a lot of excellent hockey players who never make it to the NHL because they become intimidated. And there are a lot of hockey players in the NHL who would be all-stars if they would drop their gloves and fight. But they won't, mostly because they are afraid of losing. They don't want to suffer the embarrassment of getting beaten up, or just fighting, in front of their wives and children. It's a shame, but there are many guys who fit into that category.

My third year with Boston was very exciting, and frustrating. We fought for first place all year only to surrender it to Montreal on the final weekend. Bobby Orr stayed healthy all year and started to become the best player in the game. And for the first time in a decade the Bruins won a Stanley Cup series, beating Toronto in four straight games.

We moved next into one of the most exciting Stanley Cup

series ever played. The Canadiens beat us in six games. They did it by beating us in overtime in the first two games in Montreal. In the first one, we held a 1 to 0 lead into the final minute before they tied it up and beat us in overtime. In the second game, we held a 2 to 0 lead with five minutes to play and they bounced back to catch us again and put us away in overtime.

We should have been going back to Boston with a two-game lead to finish them off. And we would have because we beat them twice in Boston handily. We played a very poor fifth game in Montreal, but should have taken the sixth in Boston. We fired 50 shots on Rogatien Vachon that night and could score only once. Jean Beliveau beat us with an excellent rising shot right under the crossbar in double overtime, and we were out of it. The best team lost that year, but an excellent Montreal team won by taking advantage of every opportunity.

My fourth and final year with the Bruins was a series of peaks and valleys. After my second year as coach, I had signed a two-year contract raising my salary from $15,000 to $20,000 the first year and $22,000 the second year. When I started the 1970 season, the last year of my contract, I wanted to see how the front office felt about me. Early in the year I approached them about a new contract. I wanted $30,000 a year. They offered me $25,000 and wouldn't change. I wondered many times if some of these people really cared for me. I heard too many times through the grapevine that they were critical of me and some of the players. So I decided no matter what, I would quit the Bruins at the end of the season.

And what a wild year it was. In training camp, Teddy Green was seriously injured in his now famous stick swinging duel with Wayne Maki, who was playing with St. Louis then. Maki started the stick part by spearing Green. Green gave him a whack back and then Maki hit Green in the head. When I saw the way Green went down, my heart went into my mouth. I knew he was hurt bad. I know a lot of our players felt then that this would cost us the Stanley Cup. Rick Smith changed their thinking when he came along and did a great job filling in for Green.

During the regular season Orr and Esposito went crazy. Bobby started to introduce the four-man rush into the offensive style of the NHL. Phil started doing his thing in the middle, showing how a center could play almost a pivot in front of the net and get great goal production out of it. Both of them scored over 100 points, with Bobby winning the scoring title and four major awards. On the last day of the season, we lost first place again, to Chicago, and it caused me to think I was snake bitten. You start to believe destiny is working against you.

In the playoffs we exploded into a great team. We had a tough series with New York before we won in six games. Then we won the next eight straight, handling Chicago and St. Louis without any trouble. All the while I knew I wouldn't be coming back. I waited for three days after we won the Cup to tell the Bruins' management of my decision. I didn't want to throw a damper on the delirious celebration the players and fans were going through in Boston. My intention was simply to walk in and tell them it was over and, before they could say anything, walk out again. I really didn't expect them to try to change my mind.

My friend Bob Woolf, one of the top sports attorneys around and just one of a half dozen people who knew of my decision, wanted me to go in and sit down with all the Bruins' brass. I told him, "Bob, this is a waste of time. I don't mean anything to these people. They don't care one damn bit about Harry Sinden."

So we went into the meeting, and when I told them about my job opportunity with Stirling-Homex in Rochester, they said "Harry, we're happy for you. We wish you all the luck in the world." Never once did they say, "Harry, can we get you to change your mind?" If they had I might have stayed. The money wasn't the big thing that made me leave. Money was only a symbol in that deal. I figured when I talked to them earlier, if they really thought anything of me they would have given me what I wanted, particularly since it wasn't a helluva lot.

I was out of hockey and into the home building business. Dave Stirling, a schoolmate of mine in Toronto, had developed a thriving company which specialized in modular housing. When I took the job at Stirling-Homex, I sincerely didn't want hockey to be a big part of my life anymore. I wanted to be a fan. I bought season tickets to the Buffalo Sabres game and listened to games on radio. While with Stirling, I received 12 offers to go back to coaching. Six came from the NHL, six from the World Hockey Association. Every one was for more money than I was making with Stirling-Homex. I didn't take any of them because I made a committment to Dave Stirling and I wanted to see it through.

Then came the first reports of this series with Russia and it really turned me on. When I studied all the possibilities, I humbly considered myself a leading contender for the job as coach. I used pure logic to make this brilliant deduction. With the series being played in September, when every pro hockey team is in training camp, who else would be available?

I sensed right away this series would become the most famous in the history of hockey, and I wanted to be part of it. I saw my name mentioned as a possibility a couple of times for the coaching job, but no one in an official capacity had contacted me. I was getting jumpy to let someone know I was available and willing to take it. Then Ron Brown, a sportswriter from Kingston, called me about it and I told him why I wanted it, and what I'd do with it. The story was carried all over Canada. Now I sat back and waited for the phone call. It didn't come.

So I had to make the call. I tried to do it without being obvious. A friend of mine at Stirling-Homex had asked me about getting his son into Bobby Orr's summer hockey camp. This gave me the opening to call Al Eagleson, who owns part of Bobby's camp, but who, more importantly for my intentions, was a key figure in the Hockey Canada organization. When I got Al on the phone he surprised me by saying, "Gee, Harry, you must have been reading my mind. I was supposed to call you a few days ago and never got around to it. Would you be interested in taking the coaching job against Russia?"

So I didn't have to take a posture I didn't want to: I never wanted to come right out and ask for the job. And it made me feel good when Eagleson told me the players—in the form of the NHL Players Association—had a meeting and wanted me as coach.

The following Sunday, June 4, I met Al in Toronto and we went over the coaching thing in complete detail. I told him how I would operate if I got the job. I told him I wanted the same salary that I was making at Stirling-Homex to make up for what I'd lose when I took a leave of absence. And I stressed that I didn't want any interference from the board. I wanted to pick the team and I wanted to run it my way.

The following Wednesday, Al called and asked me to come

to Montreal for a meeting with the steering committee of Hockey Canada. They—a nine-man board—wanted to interview me for the job. Basically, they asked me why I wanted the job and why I should get it. I told them I wanted it for the challenge and said I thought I could do the job because I had never lost to the Russians as a player; I knew the Russian style; I knew the international style of hockey; and I had proven I could win with National Hockey League players. (I heard later that Milt Schmidt, Jean Beliveau, Gordie Howe and Emile Francis were also candidates.)

After the interview, the men asked me to step out of the room. In just a few minutes, they brought me back and told me the job was mine. One thing they did question was why I wanted a 35-man squad. I told them we'd need that many because we would have to practice hard against ourselves; no one else would be playing at this time for us to compete against. Perhaps I should have brought in the 35 and cut down to 20. But I didn't want to have to cut players and have them go home with the embarrassment of not making the team. They had given up a month of their summer vacation. I didn't think it would be fair to them.

Sweden, Sept. 14

There is a classic line by Darrell Royal, head football coach at Texas, that came back to me today. Royal was asked after a losing game if Texas would have won had some of his injured stars been available. "The way I figure it," said Royal, "you have to dance with the people you brung."

That's the way I feel about it. Bobby Orr is here with us and is going to test his injured knee in the next couple of days to see if he might be ready for the Russians. Personally, I doubt it very much, but the final decision will be up to the doctors and his advisers. Bobby is still out of shape and I don't want to get him into the series just because he is Bobby Orr.

Orr's presence I guess, triggered a series of questions today which all seem to revolve around, "what if Bobby Hull was playing? Or Derek Sanderson? Or J.C. Tremblay?" Great. But they're not and they can't. So we'll dance with the people we brung, a good group of guys who, on the whole, couldn't have given any more of themselves.

Yet, the mention of Hull, Sanderson and the rest, tempts me

to take inventory of some of the things that have gone on with Team Canada. We wanted Hull, Sanderson, Gerry Cheevers and Tremblay on this team. They're not here because some of the owners in the National Hockey League didn't want them to be.

The first thing I did when I was named head coach and general manager of this team was to get John Ferguson as my assistant. I had never really met or known Fergie away from the ice, but I admired him on it, and thought he would be a great asset for the team if I could get him. We got together the next day—a meeting set up by Al Eagleson—and I was immediately impressed by him. Although he had been a rugged, battling player with the Canadiens, he was really quiet and almost shy. I also knew from the success he had made in private business after his hockey career that Ferguson was very bright. "I consider this the biggest honor ever given to me," said Fergie when we offered him the job.

Next, we sat down and selected Team Canada. In the beginning we picked the top 50 players in the NHL by choosing left wings, right wings, centers, left defensemen and right defensemen, ten deep. We picked each position one to ten, then we cut the squad to 35. It took about six "shape-ups" before we finally came up with the team.

From the 35-man original selection, Hull, Sanderson, Cheevers, Ed Giacomin and Walt Tzacsuk of the Rangers, Dallas Smith of the Bruins, and J.C. Tremblay and Jacques LaPerriere of Montreal could not make it for one reason or another. Hull, Sanderson, Cheevers and Tremblay were ruled out because they had signed contracts with the World Hockey Association. Ed Giacomin had to beg off with a knee problem. Smith is a farmer in Winnipeg and it would have cost him $7000 to leave. He has 700 acres of barley and oats, and it costs him $10 an acre during September to harvest the crop. Although we did reimburse some players for time missed at their own summer hockey schools, we couldn't pay $7000 for anyone. Tzacsuk really disappointed me. He used a hockey school as a cop out when almost every guy who came to Team Canada had the same kind of problem. LaPerriere missed it because his wife was having a baby.

But the big problem, the one that transcended all others, was the World Hockey Association lockout. Hull became the test case. Just as we were putting together the team, word leaked that he was jumping. Yet as far as John Ferguson and I were concerned Hull was going to play for Team Canada. I tried for days to reach Bobby to ask if he would be available. I finally got him after he signed with Winnipeg. Bobby said he would play, on one condition—he wanted his money from the series to go to the WHA players pension fund. I told him we'd work something out about the money, but for the time being not to say anything about it.

Well, within two days Bobby told the newspapers he was going to play for Team Canada and that his money would go to the WHA pension fund. This promptly brought a phone call from Clarence Campbell, who advised me that Bobby Hull could not play in the series because he had not signed his 1972-73 contract with an NHL team, an agreement reached between the NHL and Hockey Canada. I told Campbell that I didn't know of any such agreement and wanted Hull on the team.

"Well, just look at your own letter. It's right there," said Campbell, referring to a letter I had sent out to hockey officials with some of the regulations for players joining Team Canada.

The very first sentence in the letter—which I typed myself—stated that a player must be signed to a "standard NHL contract," for the 1972-3 season, so that he would be protected by that contract should he be injured.

I told Mr. Campbell, "Look, that wording is just force of habit. I didn't mean anything definite about an NHL contract. My feeling was that it could be any contract. What if we had a super junior like Bobby Orr? You mean to say I couldn't let him play for Team Canada because he wasn't signed to an NHL contract?"

Campbell ducked the question: "But we don't have anyone like that right now."

I would find out after, that before I got into the picture Campbell and officials of Hockey Canada had agreed to this "NHL only" situation. To this day I have never seen any proof of such an agreement in writing. All I have is their word for it. Although I've never seen it in writing, I have no reason to believe that Mr. Campbell wasn't telling the truth.

One thing that still bothers me is what happened the night I got the job. Five minutes after I was picked I was at a press conference answering questions about a job that wasn't even mine two hours before. The first or second question was about

Bobby Hull. "Would I sign Bobby Hull if he jumped to the WHA?"

Very quickly I answered "No! No way!"

Then the reporter said back, "Why not? He's a Canadian."

This made me waver for a minute before I said, "You're right. He will be eligible."

Hull's name had not come up at the meeting when I got the job, but when I corrected myself at the press conference none of the members of Hockey Canada, who were all in the room, stepped up to say "Harry, you're wrong. Hull can't play." If the agreement had been made why didn't they say so then?

At the time, I didn't think that much of it because I never thought a player of Hull's caliber would jump. In the following weeks his case became a "cause celebre." But it was really hopeless. The American owners just weren't going to go for it. Legally they couldn't afford to because they were going to court to attempt to stop the guys who jumped to the WHA from even making personal appearances for their new clubs. And they sent word that if Hull or any other "defector" played for Team Canada, the owners would pull the rest of their NHL players off the squad. We needed their permission. We Canadians, as Darrell Royal might say, were hogtied by the Americans.

Personally, I could see the Americans' view from a business end. But for the sake of hockey, which I feel should have been the paramount factor, Hull and the others should have been allowed to play. At the first meeting I had with the squad on the night we checked into training camp, almost all of the players' questions were on this topic. When I explained to them what had happened, they accepted the fact that the American owners were holding the cards.

Even the Prime Minister, Pierre Trudeau, couldn't help. If anything he hurt us. We met with him at the height of the Hull controversy and he wanted to lend his support. But we told him the best thing he could do was keep quiet about it because we hoped to reach some sort of quiet settlement with the owners. So the next day Trudeau came out publicly behind Hull. Between Trudeau and Goldsworthy it seems I'm not talking very straight these days.

Another thing that cropped up at the players meeting was the rumor that Bobby Orr and Harold Ballard, owner of the Maple Leafs, were going to make a big score by selling the TV rights to the games. But Eagleson and I explained to the players that Orr and Ballard weren't getting a dime, that their companies were simply lining up the best TV contracts for Team Canada, and they were satisfied.

Players are extremely sensitive when it comes to a dollar. When we were calling the players to see if they would like to be on the team, almost every agent wanted to know where all the money was going. A typical agent, a guy named Fred Sharf from Boston, who handles the Esposito brothers, was a real pain. You wouldn't believe how suspicious these people are. Sharf wanted to know how much Bobby Orr was making on the deal. "This whole thing is ridiculous," he said. "You're depriving my clients of a chance to make a lot of money. The Bruins and Black Hawks won't stand for this." But when I talked to Phil and Tony they were all for it—once they got the right answers.

This is a good time to square away the money situation. I'm getting $15,000 for being head coach and general manager of Team Canada. John Ferguson is making $10,000 as my assistant. Bob Haggert, with us as an administrative aide, is making $5000. Mike Cannon and Al Eagleson won't make a dime. The players aren't getting paid for any of the games against Russia. They are getting $500 per game for the six exhibitions we are playing: three intra-squad games we played in Toronto before the series started: the games we will play against the Swedish National team here Saturday and Sunday night; and the game we will play against Czechoslovakia after the Soviet series is over. So in all, a player will receive $3000 plus $17 per day expenses and a trip to Europe for him and his wife. All the profits from this series are being split evenly between Hockey Canada and the NHL Players Pension Fund. Depending on the final television figures, I would estimate the total profit will be around $1 million, with half going to Hockey Canada and the rest to pensions.

Hockey Canada is an organization set up by the Canadian government in 1969 with two purposes: to foster and support youth hockey, and to develop a national team to represent Canada in international tournaments. Its directors come from all over Canada and have wide ranging hockey backgrounds.

In pursuing the second part of this directive—to create a national team for international competition—Hockey Canada became involved with the Russians. Their negotiations were completed last spring, and I tell you without any hesitation, we were taken by the Russians. How we could ever agree to play them at this time of year—the worst possible time for Canadians—I'll never know. Why we played international rules instead of NHL rules I can't understand. I'm positive Hockey Canada gave the Russians all these concessions because they needed the money from the series. As I understand it, they are low on funds and need the cash to operate their programs.

This is why once I got the drift of what was going on I divorced myself from Hockey Canada. They didn't like it, but I thought it necessary. We didn't have enough time to have an unwieldy committee meeting every time we needed a decision.

So as soon as possible I set up what we called "Team Five" to run this series—myself, Fergie, Al Eagleson, Bob Haggert, and Mike Cannon. We're the ones who decided on the name Team Canada, which really upset the Hockey Canada people. They wanted Hockey Canada to be the name, and nothing else. They walked out of our press conference in a huff when we announced the name Team Canada. But we picked Team Canada because we felt the name should represent all of Canada, not just one organization. We also liked the fact the name was easily translated into French. The Team of Canada. That's what we are despite all the headaches.

Sweden, Sept. 15

It's definite that Orr won't play. His knee just isn't coming around. He's been skating since we got here and his knee is still tender. I would have bet a long time ago that this was going to happen. I've seen Bobby come off two other knee operations and it was the same way.

Before the Russians put us on our pants in Canada, I wasn't that upset about not having Bobby. I thought we had enough talent without him. Now I'd love to have him. To me, Orr is the only player in the world who can mean the difference between winning and losing a hockey game. He's the only player who can control the game and its tempo. He's the only player who can dominate. But where he would have really helped this team was as a leader. Orr is not only skilfull, but dedicated and inspirational. No teammate wants to look bad in front of Bobby Orr. He's so good that the guys in his team want to look good in his eyes. He makes coaching easy. How can the fringe player on your team loaf, when the greatest player in the game just goes, and goes, and goes every second he's on the ice?

A great example of this came in the final Stanley Cup game this year when Orr dominated the Rangers even though he was playing on just one good leg. You could tell he was hurting, and couldn't make his usual moves. But he has such great presence on ice that the rest of the Bruins rallied around him and played one of the most disciplined hockey games I've ever seen. Every man did his job, because they knew if they held their men in check, Bobby Orr would find a way to win it for them. And he did. The Bruins won 3 to 0 over New York and he had a hand in every goal.

Having Orr in this series would have been very interesting. I don't know whether he'd be able to control the puck against the Russians the way he does in the NHL. On the other hand, Bobby Orr is one of the few people in the history of sports whom I consider truly gifted. He brought moves to the game of hockey that no one had ever seen before. And he did these things on instinct. I don't know how many times our guys on the Bruins would say, "Geez, he does something new every day."

These little gimmicks of Orr's are just things that spill out of him when there's no other way. He gets in a jam and all of a sudden he comes up with a double pirouette, and . . . Zoom! He's flying away free. As I wonder about it now I can't help but think that the emotion, the importance, and the challenge of this Russian series would have driven Bobby Orr to greater heights. Who knows what his limits are? Every time you think he's done it all, he goes one step beyond.

Strange as it may seem, the Russians wanted very much for Orr to play. They even made an exception for him because of his injury, and allowed us to carry Orr on our roster as an extra man, and agreed to let us play him any time he was ready. I feel they wanted Orr to play against them so that they could study him and learn from him.

The Russians, as much as anything else, are using this series for an experiment. They want to find out what their limitations are. One of their officials told me when I visited Moscow in July, "We're so happy to have this series because we were getting bored by the lack of competition. This will renew our interest in the game."

Our relations with the Russians to this point have been good. The more I talk to them and get to know them, I realize that they wanted this series worse than we did, which is why we were suckers for making so many concessions to them in the first place.

I learned how badly the Russians wanted this series when the other members of "Team Five" and I took a dry run to Sweden and Russia in July. (I didn't think I'd be able to go because I had planned to spend that time doing some work for Stirling-Homex. But this hasn't exactly been my year. Stirling-Homex has gone broke. As of Oct 1, Harry Sinden won't have a job. One day our company has $65 million in sales, the next day we're out of business. It cost me a lot of money, because if that company had taken off the way I thought it was going to, I would have been in good shape financially. In retrospect, my loss with Stirling was my gain in this series because I had the time to come to Europe and meet the Russians.)

Our bon voyage from the folks at Hockey Canada was pure negativism. "You're wasting your time," we were told, "the Russians won't talk to you and they won't change anything."

The Hockey Canada people were afraid we'd screw up the series with the Russians and cost them all that money. We felt we had to get a lot of things straightened out. We needed to know if Stan Mikita, who was born a Czech, could play. Would we have to stick with the European concept of two referees? What would be the final date for naming rosters, and how big could they be? We also wanted to discover the logistical problems involved in moving a 50-man entourage around Europe, instead of finding out when it would be too late to make adjustments.

When we got to Russia, we were greeted with open arms at the airport. All the USSR's top hockey and sport officials were there, including their head coach, Bobrov. Right there at the airport these people who "wouldn't talk to us" said, "All we'll need is 10 minutes to straighten out these matters."

I told them, "If that's the way you feel, it won't even take five."

We made arrangements to meet at 10 the next morning at the newspaper Izvestia, where we had a small press conference. Since they have just one newspaper in Russia, they don't have that many sportswriters, but for this they also brought in writers from sports magazines. The first question I got hit with really made me laugh. "Why didn't you select Dave Keon of Toronto to your team?" asks this Russian through an interpreter.

Well, I nearly fell over. How the hell did this guy ever hear of Dave Keon? It was the kind of question you'd expect from some gas station attendant in Oshawa, not from a Russian sportswriter. This was the first inkling I had of how much they really knew about us, and everything we did.

The official meeting was very rewarding. They gave us everything we wanted, except a change in the refereeing. We knew they wouldn't change the fact that the series was to be played in September and under International rules. This had been a firm agreement when Hockey Canada made the original deal with the Russians. They gave us the other things—letting Mikita play; upping the roster to 35 players in Canada, 30 in Russia, and making the exception for Orr; granting us 500 extra seats for Canadians who would come to Russia for the series; and giving us additional press accomodations. The meeting didn't finish in ten minutes, but it was quick, and friendly.

When the business was out of the way, the Russians decided it was time for some toasts. Out came the vodka—Kristal vodka. There were 10 or 12 Russians and the 8 of us, including our interpreter. It became a helluva luncheon thanks to the Kristal. The Russians were so pleased that they wanted to toast everyone. We learned that the custom is for each man to toast everyone else. The Russians would toast one of our players . . . or our officials . . . or Canada. We'd have to do the same thing for them.

"Bobby Orr." Zip! Over the gums. No ice. No mix. No nothing. Straight vodka.

"Valeri Kharlamov." Same thing. Straight.

I'll say this about Kristal—after a few it doesn't seem all that bad. Our embassy officials and our interpreter said they had never seen the Russians so open and friendly about everything. It was a very nice session, with hockey the main course. (I wish I had known about Kristal when I was coaching the Bruins. I would have sent a case to Fergie before each game). Fergie and Bobby Haggert were the first to go. They both slept for 16 straight hours.

This had been my first real meeting with Soviet officials and I was impressed with their attitude about hockey. I asked one of the Ministers of Sport: "What's the number one sport in Russia?"

"Hockey," he answered. "Hockey is 1½ times more popular than any other sport. We have three million people playing hockey in the Soviet Union." In Canada, we have something like 250,000, and we think that's a lot.

Our negotiations that day incorporated the exchange of scouts. We'd send two to Russia to watch their team before the series, they'd send a couple to Canada. Their scouts, who arrived while we were in training camp, were two of their coaches, Kulagin and Cherneshev. These men were what you would expect, totally dedicated. They watched every practice we had, taking page after page of notes. One day I had the players in the middle of the ice just talking about practice times or something when I looked up and spotted them writing like hell. All I could conceive of them writing was, "Sinden now has players in middle of ice." I mean, there wasn't anything else they could have been writing that fast about at the moment. Those two guys didn't miss a trick. I had to laugh when the Russians came to practice in Montreal and were using a couple of drills Team Canada had been using.

After Kulagin and Cherneshev had been in Canada three or four days, they invited us up to their hotel room to talk hockey. They were a contrast in personalities. Kulagin was deadly serious, Cherneshev was a jovial, have-another-vodka type. Cherneshev whipped out the Kristal and after four toasts and a can of caviar, we had a great bull session about hockey.

I guess knocking four quick vodkas down the hatch makes for agreeable meetings and this pleased Mr. Cherneshev no end. He didn't think there could be any more hospitable way for us to exchange ideas. He was very nice and I was impressed with both of them. During this meeting we discovered they knew everything about our players. They told us they had made a complete "book" on every one of our players. They said they were impressed with our practice sessions, and confided they didn't think we would be able to control such "stars" of the sport the way we did.

But they also had questions. "Why don't you practice like we do in Russia? We work out from nine to 11 in the morning and then bring the team back at six for another workout."

I told them their method made more sense, but that traditionally no one works morning and night, and that our men would never go for it. In Russia, we learned, a player practices two hours on the ice in the morning; eats lunch; sleeps; and comes back refreshed for night practice.

"How much work do your players do outside the arena?" the Russian coaches asked. "Do they use the trampoline? Do your men tumble? Play soccer or basketball? What kind of weight training program do you have?"

They went on to explain how complete their program is. All their players have to be highly skilled at other sports—gymnastics, soccer, basketball—and they work out in the gym periodically to keep these skills at a high level. They use the trampoline and practice tumbling to develop overall agility. Soccer conditions their foot movement so they can control the puck better on skates. Basketball is used to improve hand and eye movement, as well as to develop the pass patterns similar to the ones they use on the ice. And the weight training is for overall strength. In my estimation, a Russian who weighs 170 is as strong as a Canadian who weighs 185. This additional strength comes from his rigorous training and conditioning.

Our scouts, Bob Davidson and John McLellan of the Toronto Maple Leaf organization, weren't as fortunate in Russia. When they arrived in Moscow the Soviet team had not yet formed. Most of the players were with their individual teams in different parts of the country playing a tournament. As a result, Davidson and McLellan were limited. Except for watching the Red Army team, which had about 15 players who would eventually make the Russian squad, our scouts had to watch several different games with just one or two players who would play against us. Only at one practice session did they have the opportunity to see the entire Russian team together.

Davidson and McLellan were abused in Canada when the Russians beat us. They had said publicly when they returned from the Soviet Union that we wouldn't have any trouble beating the Russians. So when the Russians socked it to us in the opener, they were natural targets. This was unfair. Sure, they underestimated the Russians—we all did. But they did bring us back the information we wanted and good reports on most of their top players, and they were only there for six days.

The only thing that was off in the scouting report was the assessment of the Russian goalie, Tretiak. Davidson and McLellan saw him play just one night and he was terrible. His team was beaten 8 to 1 and Tretiak was dismal. As we found out too late, the game took place on the eve of his wedding, so he probably didn't have his mind on the action. But there wasn't any way for our scouts to know the guy was just shook up. All they could go by was what they saw.

The Russian scouts, meanwhile, have been with us ever since. Not even James Bond got this kind of coverage. But I've enjoyed our discussions and I think they have also. I know one guy who really got a kick out of our meeting in Canada with the Kristal and caviar was the interpreter. It turned out he is a real hockey fan. I wondered at the end of the meeting what part of the Canadian government he worked for.

"Oh, me?" he said, in English. "I don't work for the government. I make peanut butter at Canada Packers."

Sweden, Sept. 16

This is a great place for a holiday, but not for hockey. We played our first game in Europe tonight and beat the Swedes 4 to 1 in a rotten game. Every Canadian team who has come over here before has had trouble, and now we're having ours. These guys are sneaks, and dirty hockey players. If we had to play them eight times like we do the Russians, it would be a bloodbath. But there's only one left tomorrow night and maybe we slowed them down in this game tonight.

They were laying in the weeds for us. We set up this part of the Team Canada tour for two reasons. First, we wanted to get used to playing on the larger surfaces they have in Europe. Second, we wanted a rest for our players before we faced the grind of four games in Russia, knowing that wasn't going to be much fun for them. From what they showed me tonight the Swedes are good, but not in the same league with the Russians, although we had to put out to beat them.

We won this game because the Swedes were a little in awe of us. In the first period we were absolutely terrible. It was the worst period of hockey we've played since we put the team together. As the game wore on we got stronger and started to take command. Henderson, Clarke, Cashman and Parise got the goals for us.

We seemed to adjust to the bigger surface in the second and third periods, but there was no way we could adjust to the officials. We had two West Germans—Baader and Kompalla—and they were absolutely terrible. They couldn't even skate. They were miles behind the play all night and don't know the damn rules. Their incompetence helped the game become very bitter.

I think the Swedes geared themselves for a rough game, playing against the NHL stars. But they don't know what a rough game is by our standards. Their way of handling it is to get rough from behind, never from in front. Right from the faceoff they were spearing, holding, interfering and, most of all, backstabbing. (That's a term we use in the NHL for a check delivered directly from behind that takes a player into the boards face first.) You don't do this in the NHL unless you're looking for a fight. It's our custom to let a player go into the corner for the puck without jamming his face into the boards. You allow him to turn one way or another before you make your hit.

The Swedes kept backstabbing our players all night and our guys did the obvious in retaliation. We didn't try to be cute about it: we just swung around and let the guy have it with a cross-check. Of course, the officials seemed intent on showing the Canadians they weren't going to be intimidated by any of the antics of these professionals. We started getting the majority of the penalties, when in almost every instance it was a cheap shot that triggered the reaction. We never would have tolerated it in Canada.

Like the Russians, the Swedes proved to be great ones for interfering. We're learning this is a fact of life in European play.

Because there are only two officials instead of three, the Europeans are able to pull off this crap behind the officials' backs. Our guys just aren't used to this kind of play, and we're not going to accept it either. After the first period I told them not to take any guff from these people. If they pull something we don't like, it should be answered the same way it would in the National Hockey League.

I could tell by the way the Swedes,—the players, the coaches and the fans—reacted, that they wanted desperately to beat us. But we're not ready for it. How can I ask our guys to pysche themselves up for games that are really supposed to be just practice sessions? I tried to talk to the officials during the first and second periods but it was hopeless. They behaved as if we were cry babies, complaining because we weren't playing well. The referees, the Germans, understood English.

Maybe something was lost in translation, but I'm sure they got the drift of what I was telling them. In the second period one of them, Baader, came over to the bench to talk to me. This is never done in the National Hockey League. One of our guys had just been speared and I was complaining as heatedly as I could. Baader told me he was going to give me a bench penalty, and he should have, because I shouldn't have been talking that way to an official. But I was frustrated. So were the players. They'd take a cheap shot from a Swede, give one back, and then be ready to fight. But the Swedes wouldn't fight, and we'd end up in the penalty box.

My outrage at the officials reached a peak in the second period when Phil Esposito was given a minor. On the way to the box Phil shoved one of the Swedish players. Another minor. All of a sudden Espo was tagged with a ten-minute misconduct on top of this because the referee made a mistake. He confused spearing, which you can assess a misconduct for, with cross-checking. He had called cross-checking on Phil and then gave him a misconduct for it. So we lost Phil for ten minutes because they didn't know their own international rules. And these guys are supposed to be two of the best in Europe.

So it was a rough night for us. We didn't want to lose and we didn't want the Swedes to think they could intimidate us. We needed the win because we hadn't won since Toronto and it would really put us down to be beaten by Sweden.

The play of the Ratelle line was another disappointment. We put it back together hoping the Ranger's trio could find themselves. But they didn't play well at all. The Swedes, just like the Russians, were all over them and harried them into mistakes. I thought the bigger ice surface might let them play their own game, but it didn't work. Overall, we played poorly. Tony Esposito gave us a good game in net, and the fact that we came on a little stronger in the last two periods saved us. Mentally, we just weren't prepared to play this kind of game. This trip was supposed to be a bonus, fun and games. It's turned out to be anything but that.

During the day we received a call from Frank Mahovlich's doctor telling us that Frank can rejoin the team. His doctor thinks Frank has calmed down enough to help us in one or two games in Russia. If he seems okay when he gets here tomorrow I'll start working him with Cournoyer and Ratelle. I haven't been able to find a center for Frank and Yvan yet, but maybe Ratelle can fit with them.

I'm glad Frank didn't make it here tonight. When we got back to The Grand Hotel following the game, we found it surrounded by police. Someone had phoned a local TV station with a bomb threat. The police kept us waiting outside for two hours before they completed the search and let us in. No bomb was found, but I wondered how Frank would have felt if he pulled up to find all those cops looking for a live bomb.

Sweden, Sept. 17

I've seen a lot of terrible things happen on the ice during a hockey game. I remember when Claude Ruel, former coach of the Canadiens, lost his eye when he was accidentally struck by a stick. I saw Mickey Redmond's father, a teammate of mine with the Whitby Dunlops, nearly die one night on the ice when he accidentally got hit in the throat with a stick. He couldn't talk or breathe. His head started to swell because his windpipe was broken. Luckily, they rushed him to the hospital and saved his life with an emergency tracheotomy. And I saw Ted Green get his skull bashed in by Wayne Maki.

But not even those incidents were as vicious as the one tonight in our second and, thank God, last game with the Swedes. Ulf Sterner, a Swede who had played in Canada for a couple of years and was known as a chicken, nearly skewered Wayne Cashman's tongue. He did it deliberately. There are no two ways about it. Granted, we didn't play a totally clean game. Near the end Vic Hadfield cross checked their captain, Sjoberg, across the nose, knocking him to the ice and drawing blood. Hadfield got five minutes for high sticking, and Sjoberg got two stitches. But Sterner didn't get a thing for nearly making Cashman mute. If I had my way, no Canadian would ever play hockey in Sweden again.

The game ended in a 4 to 4 tie, but it really wasn't a game at all. Though it wasn't as rough as many of the NHL games I've seen over the years—it still was upsetting. These referees are just so bad that this kind of thing has to happen. I came over here convinced that hockey would be a much better game without fighting. Now I know I'm wrong. Clarence Campbell has maintained over the years that fighting is a necessary evil in hockey. I thought he was wrong and that fighting just made the NHL style more exciting. But he was right, and I give him credit. If we didn't fight there would be mayhem. I'm convinced of that. If the Swedes would drop their sticks they'd soon get over all the backstabbing and sneak stuff they employ.

But they don't have the guts to drop their sticks and fight. They just get in a sneak shot and take off. This thing with Cashman was really a jolt, especially coming from Sterner who we know is, shall we say, a careful hockey player. I saw it happen, but I didn't find out until later what I had really seen. Sterner was along the boards when Cashman closed in to check him. When Cash was about six feet away Sterner forgot the puck, brought up his stick, and jabbed it right in Cashman's mouth. It was a very professional job. He didn't cut Cash's lip or break any teeth. He simply hit the tongue dead center, opening a horrible gash that measured two inches long and went nearly through the tongue from top to bottom. I saw Cash flinch, then wheel away and stagger back to the bench. You could tell he was in pain but we didn't see any blood. He tried to talk but it hurt too much. Finally, our team physician, Jim Murray, pulled Wayne's mouth open and I nearly vomited on the spot. His tongue was just dangling. Cash wanted to get back at Sterner badly and tried to go after him. But the pain was too great. We sent him to the dressing room to be stitched. I couldn't believe there wasn't a penalty.

At the end of the second period, I waited on the runway for the referees. Both teams and the officials used the same runway, and in this case that resulted in a bad scene. I jumped all over the Germans verbally, telling them how unfair they were; how they were protecting the Swedes; and how they were calling only the obvious. About this time the Swedish coach, a wise guy named Svensson, made a crack to Phil Esposito, calling him chicken. "Get away from me, you fag!" Phil yelled, and gave Svensson a shove. Then the Swedish goalie, a tough guy behind a mask, said something and one of our players went after him. It quickly became ugly. Cashman, dressed in street clothes, wanted to get back at someone. We were all incensed now and Sterner and his teammates disappeared quickly. Our guys were still jawing at the referees when Fergie and I finally moved in to calm things down and get them into the dressing room.

We were still cursing each other back and forth when, like

vultures, the Swedish photographers swooped down on us. We could see by the coverage of our first game that they loved this kind of stuff: the Canadian "gangsters" caught in sequence beating up the innocent little Swedish victims. Our players who had not dressed for the game were also in the runway and, when they saw what was happening, they started grabbing the cameras. The Swedish police, complete with dogs, came to the rescue, so we hustled all our people out of the runway and into the room. It was a mess that I knew would spill over into the third period and I didn't want that to happen.

I didn't want to lose this hockey game. We were leading 2 to 1 at the time, but playing poorly. If it hadn't been for an un- believable job by Eddie Johnston in goal, we would have been buried in the first period. They were all over Eddie in that first 20 minutes, drilling many shots at him from point blank range. I had expected something like this might happen, but not quite the way it did. Fergie and I had some tough decisions to make for this one. We had an obligation to the players who hadn't skated in any games to play them here. We had to get these same players some work on the larger ice surface so they would be accustomed to it in case we needed them in Russia. And we wanted to keep our lineup tough enough to beat the Swedes, who weren't in awe of us tonight, like they were last night.

Playing a more relaxed brand of hockey, Sweden started threatening from the opening faceoff. Hadfield put us in front 1 to 0 in the first period with a 40-foot slap shot, but the game never settled down to hockey. The Swedes started their antics and we retaliated. Naturally, we were the fall guys. The people didn't see the Swedish sneak shots, they just saw the Canadian "gangsters" attack. The referees went along, giving us eight penalties for 31 minutes compared to two for the Swedes.

I always thought it took two to fight. Between the second and third period, I saw how things were shaping up. When we got settled in the dressing room I told the players, "Listen, it's foolish to continue playing like this. I know it's not your fault, but these referees just aren't going to listen to us. We're simply going to have to calm down for 20 minutes and win this hockey game. Try to avoid any trouble if you can."

We couldn't hold the lead, or our tempers. The third period was played just like the others. Fortunately, we got the tie, but ironically, it was due to the gross incompetence of the officials. The Swedes, outplaying us, took a 4 to 3 lead into the final minute and had us in a bad way. They were on the power play when Phil Esposito got the puck, moved into the Swedish end, and let go with a 35-footer. It was a good shot, but should have been handled. The Swedish defensemen, in their desperation not to let Phil get in too close, backed in on their own goalie and were actually tangled up with him when Phil let his shot go. Believe me, when I say I was thrilled with a tie. I just wouldn't be able to stomach their gloating if they beat us.

The third period contained another bad incident, and I knew we'd pay for it in the papers. Late in the game one of the Swedes ran Vic Hadfield into the boards from behind. Vic was so mad he came right back out in front of the net and decked Sjoberg, who went down in a heap in typical Swedish fashion, playing to the fans in the stands who were now whistling and screaming at us. Vic got five minutes, and Sjoberg got the Oscar. He got up slowly and managed to skate around the rink making sure everyone saw the blood before going over to his coach for sympathy. He posed for a few pictures in black and white, and then six or seven in color, before slowly skating off to get his two stitches.

Oh, yes. You wonder how the referees cost the Swedes the game? It's simple. We were offside on the tying goal. Amazing, isn't it? After trying so hard for two full games to make things easier for the Swedes, in the end the officials cost the Swedes what they wanted so desperately—a win over us.

After the game, the talk around the locker room was that we should never play here again. No one from the NHL will anyway, I'm sure of that. I was satisfied with the tie, but still infuriated after the game. After telling my players not to lose their cool, I lost mine. To this point, we never allowed the press into the dressing room after a game because it would be just too congested. We had at least 100 writers with us at all times and it would be impossible to let them all into the room at once. But tonight I was livid so I opened the door and yelled sarcastically to the press: "Okay, fellas, come on in and see the animals eat their peanuts."

It took me a long time to shake off my resentments. When we got back to the hotel, I met with Fergie, mostly for some words of encouragement, I guess. I thought, "Maybe it's me, or us, or something. Are we really the bad guys in this thing?"

After we went over all that happened to us in the past 48 hours we came to several conclusions. One, refereeing will be our biggest problem in Moscow. Two, if we don't start playing better, we're going to lose. Three, what happened here could bring us closer together as a team, and in the final result, might be a blessing in disguise—although it's difficult for me to associate this nightmare with any type of blessing.

Sweden, Sept. 18

When I selected the name for this team—Team Canada—I did so because I wanted a name that would reflect a total commitment of our country to this team. In picking the squad, we took pains to make sure that every area of our nation would be represented. I felt that if we were going to represent Canada, then all of Canada should have some feeling for this team.

Tonight I can sit here and say I truly believe we don't represent all Canadians any more. All day long, myself, Fergie and all of the players have been brought up to date by phone calls from home relating how a large segment of the population has quit on us. Not only that, but the media, both the papers and TV commentators, attack us as if we're over here on some kind of orgy, with no regard for the task at hand. They've joined with the Swedes—and the rest of the Europeans, for that matter—in labeling us bullies, gangsters, and animals. In short, some Canadians are baling out on us. I imagine that's to be expected. After looking so bad in Canada and here, they're getting themselves set for the Russians beating us in Moscow. Then they can say, "I told you so." I bet these are the same guys who picked us to whip through these people in Europe without any trouble. It's always the big talkers who choke first on their own hot air. All of this just leaves me with the feeling that Team Canada is now just a group of 50 guys who are going to have to pull together and protect their flanks. That's what our followers are doing to protect themselves. We'll have to do the same to keep from falling apart.

I can't let this second guessing start among the players. It's already hit some of the people with us in the Canadian contingent, and I don't like it. Last night, for example, I had to straighten out our team doctor Jim Murray. He's a good guy, but he's getting a little hysterical. When I went to check with him about Cashman's tongue, instead of being concerned about that, he started by asking me, "What the hell way are we playing hockey out there?" It was ludicrous. Here he was, supposedly examining one of our guys with his tongue slit open, and instead he's knocking our style. You'd think from the way Murray was carrying on that Cashman fell on his own stick. When I heard that Dr. Murray had given the same routine to Dale Tallon, I took the good doctor aside and told him what I thought. He was man enough to apologize to Tallon, a super kid who should be praised for having the character to be part of this team when he knows there is little chance of playing.

The Swedish papers didn't miss their golden opportunity. We played right into their hands. One paper had two huge photos of Sjoberg, their fallen hero. In one, the blood is running down his nose during the game. In the other, he's sitting at home with his baby resting on his knee recuperating from the two stitch cut on his nose. Another picture spread captured it all. They've got a dozen pictures, all with a Canadian assaulting a Swede. Each has a one line label. "Spearing." "Slashing." "Holding." The whole bit.

Let me bring you up to date on something else that happened today, and we'll try to get things back into proper perspective. When this trip was formed, it was agreed that we would take part of our team to a small town—Sodertalje—some 30 miles from here. There's a Volkswagen plant there and the company hired the nearby ice arena so the employees could watch us practice. I took half the squad by bus, and there were about 4000 people in the arena, many of them youngsters. We worked out for one hour and 20 minutes. Then they brought out their pee-wee teams, youngsters 12 and 13, to play a mock game against us. The guys were great. We opened by having Dionne, our little center, face off against their little center and the crowd roared with laughter. Later, Guy Lapointe did a great job playing a drunken sailor on skates, weaving up and down the ice. Many of our players clowned around with the kids, gave autographs, and worked individually with them giving tips. I was proud of our players. They could easily have been bitter at anything Swedish, but they were real pros. People might be jumping off our bandwagon in Canada, but I'll bet the people of Sodertalje are in our corner.

This practice seemed to perk our guys up. On the way back I threw some beer on the bus and we started singing songs like a bunch of kids. It was nice. It made the guys forget their problems for awhile. I thought I sensed a good feeling on that bus. We are coming closer together. In Canada, as we moved from city to city playing games, the players still had their own friends in those places. Now they're starting to be buddy-buddy with each other over here, going out together for a few beers after practice and having some fun together at night.

We've had an 11 o'clock curfew on this trip the night before games. I caught two guys out the other night, but they were back by 11:30 so I'm not going to make a big deal out of it. How can I? I can't fine them. I have to depend on their good judgment and the respect they might have for Fergie and me to get them to abide by the rules. To date, we haven't had any problems, despite all the phony stories about guys staying out all hours of the night, which, I understand, are being spread around back home. These guys haven't acted any differently than if they were in Detroit, or Chicago, or Buffalo. (Well, maybe Buffalo's stretching the point a bit.)

But I know one guy who isn't out having fun tonight— Wayne Cashman. He's in the hospital with his tongue so swollen he can hardly breathe. He can't eat or talk. Not being able to breathe won't bother Cash as much as not being able to eat or talk. He's being fed intravenously, which is not his style. Cash loves his chow.

A couple of months after the Bruins won the Stanley Cup in 1970, Cash was still celebrating. As I understand it through the Boston grapevine, Wayne became rather vociferous on this occasion and was asked by the law enforcement agency of a particular suburban town to lodge with them for the evening. Cash went quietly, and at the station showed his knowledge of the law when he requested the one phone call allowed in such situations.

The wish was granted by his hosts, who thought Cashman was phoning for legal assistance. Thirty minutes later, a taxi pulled up to the station and the driver approached the officer on duty with $10 worth of Chinese food from a nearby takeout restaurant for one Mr. Wayne Cashman.

He's settling for Swedish soup through a tube right now.

Sweden, Sept. 19

Our players must be superhuman. Today we had the best practice session we've had together and it proved that, contrary to public opinion, we are in much better physical condition than the Russians. Let's face it. Could the Russians stay out all night drinking and carousing like our guys do and still skate their butts off the next day? Never. Only NHL players can do that. Once, during the Canadian part of this trip, a writer asked me how I thought a Russian player would stand up in the NHL. Kiddingly, I told him, "I wouldn't be able to tell until I saw how he could handle some swinging spot like Brandy's or The Point After in Boston." This is all just tongue in cheek today. It must be that I feel good about the way our team was flying today in practice. We gave them the most strenuous skating drills we've had and they were dragging when they left the ice, but they seemed happy. We're in better shape than we were at home.

It strikes me that maybe the players relish going to Moscow as the underdog. Despite the lousy experiences we endured in the games here, my guess is we'll benefit in the long run by the way the players are starting to like one another. Making a *team* has been our aim since the first day. In training camp in Toronto we purposely set up the dressing rooms to discourage the formation of cliques. We didn't let two players from any one team sit side by side. We gave privileges in this regard only to the players from the Maple Leafs. We let them use the same lockers they use with the Toronto team. As we were choosing the players, we scratched any guy who was a known troublemaker, unless he was so super we couldn't afford to leave him off. Even so, if there were such a player, and he became a problem, he'd be gone immediately because we felt we had to have harmony to win.

I was most apprehensive about the way players from the Bruins would be accepted by the other players from around the league. To put it bluntly, the rest of the NHL dislikes the Bruins very much. This is partly my fault, because the rough game we developed when I was in Boston doesn't win many friends from the other side. We knew, for example, that Brad Park and Phil Esposito didn't like each other at all. Park was very critical of Espo and the rest of the Bruins in a book he authored last year. These criticisms opened some wounds which festered during the season. I remember one important game in Boston when the Rangers were trying to close ground on the first place Bruins. Park and John McKenzie got into a fight in the corner and Phil interceded. Park and McKenzie went to the box for five minutes for fighting. Phil went to the dressing room for the night as the "third man in." Phil was outraged and directed his wrath at Park, who sat in saintly fashion in the penalty box. "You know why everyone in the league hates your guts?" Phil screamed at Park. "Because you're a no good !& + $?, that's why." Park broke into his big toothless grin and waved bye-bye to Phil. After the game someone asked Esposito what he thought of Park. "Just spell his name backwards and you've got the story," said Phil.

We haven't had that kind of thing with Team Canada. If there is any animosity, it hasn't come into the open. Fergie and I noticed in our scrimmages and exhibition games in Canada that all of the players were deliberately avoiding any rough play or tough checking which might have caused a fight and divided the team. Not once in practice or anywhere else have there been any bad words among the players. I thought from the first game in Canada that we were a *team*, as I know a team to be.

But we really weren't. You really don't have a team until the players go through something which forces them to band together even tighter. Putting on the same jerseys doesn't make a team. You're still just a collection of individuals until you find a common goal.

Our own people deserting us, and the Europeans picking away at us, have given us a common cause. At the meeting we had this afternoon Al Eagleson brought this point home well. The object of the meeting was to prepare our players for the logistical and other problems they might expect in Russia. Al, who handled most of the meeting, pointed out that the rooms would probably be bugged; that the players would be under constant surveillance by secret police, the KGB; that the food and hotel would not be the same as we were used to at home or in Sweden; that their wives would be joining them in Moscow and might not like the accommodations, but would have to put up with them and not let it interfere with the series. We warned them against two other things: exchanging money in the streets or anywhere in Russia, for it is considered a very serious offense; also, there would be 3000 Canadians in Moscow, most of them in our hotel, so we advised the men not to become too involved with them. We didn't want to ignore the people from back home, yet we couldn't spend our time socializing and expect to win hockey games. The players didn't have any beefs. They were in full agreement with us.

The meeting was sort of emotional. Much of the discussion centered on the way we were apparently being deserted by many people back home and some of the ones with us. It was decided right here, no matter what happened, the 50 of us were going to hang tough together. "We're all in the boat together," Eagleson told the players, "so we're going to have to row to shore together. We can't bank on anyone else helping us."

I got up and gave the same kind of remarks. "Some people have dug a hole for us but we're not going to let them bury us. We'll divorce ourselves from the people who have given up on us and get the job done our way. We're improving every day and when we come up to that first game in Russia we'll be ready."

5
Game Five

Moscow, Sept. 20

Apparently, the Russians are going to play the part of gracious hosts. When I was here in July on our dry run, I was worried how things would go when the entire team was here. When we arrived at seven tonight, they made it as easy as they could. We were whisked right through customs, which generally isn't the custom, and the set-up at the hotel was a pleasant surprise. Our headquarters will be the Intourist Hotel, where many of the other 3000 Canadians who came to Russia for the series are staying. The fans got here a day before us and didn't waste any time sampling the vodka, or champagne, which is excellent. When we hit the lobby of the hotel it was jam packed with Canadians enjoying themselves.

The wives of the players and officials were here when we arrived. Although they were tired from the long trip, and lost two hours going through time zones, the guys were excited about seeing some "friendly" faces from home (at least we didn't think the wives had copped out yet). One of my first moves in the hotel was to check out the dining room and our private team room. Both were excellent and I was sure the

Russians were going to do everything they could to make our stay here as pleasant as possible. The team had steak for dinner and it was prepared well. The Soviets, as they prefer to be called, assigned some chefs to us for our stay here and they seem willing to give us what we want. We brought 300 steaks with us from Canada which we want to set aside for our pregame meals. On the whole the quality of the Russian food is far below what we're accustomed to. After dinner I went up to the room which is rather drab, not furnished with any modern flavor at all. I do have a sitting area separate from the sleeping area, so that makes it a suite over here.

I'm pleased at the way the Russians have things organized. These games are going to be hard enough without running into any unexpected problems that would be difficult to resolve in a country like this.

However, I can't shake the feeling that we're in for a rough trip with the referees. I don't say that they appear partial to the Europeans. They just seem to have it in for these rough Canadian pros they've heard so much about, and seem determined, in Sweden anyway, to show us we can't get away with anything. Another thing I don't like about the refereeing is the 'axe' the Russians have hanging over their heads. Next year, 1973, the World Championships are going to be played in Moscow. The chairman of the selection committee for the World Championships is a Russian who is very involved in our series, Mr. Sterevoitov. All the officials being used in this series are international ice hockey referees for whom the most prestigious professional honor is to be selected to work in the World Championship. Mr. Sterevoitov will make the choices for the next one and, frankly, I don't like something he pulled with the officials while we were in Canada.

Before I was picked for this job, the Canadian Amateur Hockey Association reached an agreement with the Russians that international referees, not pro officials, would be used exclusively in this series. At my conference with the Russians here in July, I wanted to change this. I played under the international system, and it's definitely inferior. Only two officials are used and both are considered referees with equal authority. I don't think you can handle a game with two bosses. There has to be one who can make the final decision. In the NHL three officials are used: the referee has the final say, the other two are linesmen who just look for offside and icing. This frees the referee to watch for penalties.

Under the international system, both referees are responsible for all three duties—calling penalties, offsides and icings. As a result, they try so hard to get up ice to call the offside properly, they miss what is going on behind them. On top of this, international referees are generally inferior skaters, when, if anything, they should be superior skaters. Because of this, I knew they wouldn't be able to keep up with the NHL style of play. These feelings were confirmed in Canada during the first four games, and reconfirmed in Sweden. Their biggest drawback is not catching what is going on behind them. The Europeans are smart enough to understand that they can get away with interference in certain situations, and they take advantage every time such a situation arises.

What I call the "human factor" is also more prevalent among international referees. In the games I was involved in as a player, it never failed that one referee would start out the game asserting himself and making all of the calls. And, just as surely, the other referee would be trying to assert himself by making more calls. This breeds a contest between the two officials over who is going to be boss. The one referee system eliminates this. The NHL referee knows who is boss, and he doesn't have to blow his whistle for recognition.

I hope these guys can shape up in this series and start calling interference. The Russians are masters at it. If one of them is late coming back up ice he'll make sure that your last guy coming up ice on the attack, usually the trailer, won't get into the play. He'll interfere with him behind the referee's back, which, of course, is completely illegal. The Russians also get away with interference in the offensive zone, which is right in front of the referees. They do this particularly well when they have the power play advantage. They'll send one of their men in near the net to set up a block on one of the defensemen, using what is known as a "pick" in basketball. Then one of their open men breaks for the net to take a pass behind this illegal "pick"!

I talked to the referees about this in Canada and in Sweden, and they acted like I didn't know what I was talking about. Evidently, they've let the Russians get away with this kind of thing so many times in international games, that they haven't got the guts to start calling it the way it's written in the rule book.

In July, during our meeting with Bobrov, Kulagin, and

Sterevoitov, we agreed to the four American officials who would work the games in Canada, and the four people who would work the games here—the two West Germans; Dahlberg, a Swede; and Bata, a Czech. For the Canadian part of the series, the Russians insisted on two Americans—Lee and Gagnon—being among the four used in North America. I didn't know it then but the Russians had had a great deal of success in international play with Lee and Gagnon working their games. At that point we didn't really care who refereed, so they picked the eight referees to be used.

The referees were to be used during specific games in North America and Europe like this: in both places, they would be lettered A, B, C, and D. A and B in Canada turned out to be Lee and Gagnon, who worked the game in Montreal which the Soviets won 7 to 3. This meant that the other two referees, C and D, worked the next game, which we won 4 to 1 in Toronto.

What I didn't know until we reached Vancouver was that after the game in Toronto Sterevoitov raced into the officials' room and flew into a rage. He called the two officials every name in the book, kicking over chairs in the dressing room as he did it. He made it plain that he was angry with their work.

In Moscow in July, we had agreed that after the first two games, a conference would be held to pick the officials for games three and four. We would try to cooperate on who we thought were the best two of the four who had worked. If we couldn't agree, then in Canada we had the choice of officials for game 3, and in game 4, Bobrov would choose for Russia. The same format will be used in Russia.

In Canada, the Russians reneged and we let them get away with it. Hindsight is 20-20, but it tells me we shouldn't have done it. Following the second game, when I still wasn't aware of Sterevoitov's little tantrum, the Russians said they wanted Lee and Gagnon for game 3. They also asked for them again in game four even though it was our choice in game 3. We let them have their way because they kept telling us in a nice way that if we truly wanted to play this series in the spirit of sportsmanship and friendship, then we should play the part of the perfect hosts and consent to their wishes.

I know one thing right now, the West Germans are going to be used very little in this half of the series. I'm going to insist on it. I don't know how good the Czech is, or the Swede, but I learned first hand how incompetent the Germans are in

Sweden and I'm not especially looking forward to seeing them again. I'm sure they have a chip on their shoulder against us after what happened.

This sport, I think, is the easiest to lose your poise in. There are so many factors to be aware of that you're constantly on edge. It's probably the only game where a player has to wonder before the contest if he's going to get into a fight. It's a game where you can get hurt at any moment by an object whizzing around at over 100 miles per hour. It's one of the few games where a player carries a lethal weapon in his hand. You have the possibility of falling down on, or being cut by, skates. The game is played on the hardest playing surface of them all, and inside boards which can cause serious injuries. Put these possibilities together and you have the most dangerous team sport in existence. We can handle that part of it, but we can't handle officials who are suspect. I know it's foolish to waste time worrying about things you can't control. Yet we have to prepare for everything. We don't want our players constantly hassling with the referees when their energies should be spent against the toughest opponents in the world.

Moscow, Sept. 21

Remember the 50-man crew we had rowing the boat ashore? Well, today we lost three of them. They jumped overboard like rats that didn't want to drown with the ship. They're not gone yet. Unfortunately, we have to wait until early tomorrow morning to get them out of here. It's not soon enough, but it's the best we can do. I had no idea this was going to happen, but once the pieces started to fit together I was stupid not to have seen the writing on the wall.

It started out to be a routine day. We had breakfast at 8:30, and then boarded two buses that took us out to the rink, about 15 minutes from the hotel. It was an interesting trip for the players who got their first look at the city in daylight.

At the arena we found everything in good shape. The dressing area is made up of three separate rooms, including a huge coaches' office. When we walked into the room we found a table with a dozen bottles of mineral water and a supply of apples and grapes. Our players got a laugh out of the "community swimming hole". I guess it's supposed to be a king size whirlpool bath. It's about the size of a small swimming pool.

The water is dirty and the players found it about as inviting as a dip in polluted Lake Erie.

When we went out on the ice to practice we noticed it was very thick—about three inches. At home the ice is never more than three-quarters of an inch thick. Thicker ice usually chips off near the top and isn't as smooth. We also noted that they used mesh fence behind the net instead of the glass we're used to seeing in the NHL. "You wait and see," said Peter Mahovlich, "that mesh is going to cost someone a goal. The puck has to take crazy bounces when it comes off of that thing." It was like a new toy for the players. Before practice they stood shooting pucks off the screen from different angles to see how they would react. The stands were filled with spectators, all men. After asking around, we learned that the Russians were having a coaching seminar in conjunction with the opening game of the series and had invited coaches to Moscow from all across the country. I didn't mind. They couldn't discover any more about us than they already knew. Hell, from the way they're supposed to have the place bugged, we couldn't keep any secrets anyhow. (Fergie and I looked all over the coaches' office for the bug. No luck. I'm afraid we wouldn't make very good spies.)

When the players finished getting the feel of the ice I called them together in the middle of the ice to tell them how I wanted my lines and defensive pairings set up. We had a number of line rushes in our workout because I wanted to make sure the men knew who they were skating with since we had made some changes.

I set up the team exactly the way I intend to play the first game here tomorrow night. Clarke will center for Ellis and Henderson. With Cashman out, I'm moving Gilbert onto right wing with Esposito and Parise. Frank Mahovlich skated well in two workouts in Sweden so he'll play with Cournoyer and Ratelle. Peter Mahovlich and Gilles Perreault are my spare forwards. The defensive pairings will be Park and Bergman, White and Stapleton, Seiling and Lapointe. I would have played Savard instead of Seiling but his ankle, which he fractured in Winnipeg, still isn't ready yet.

The rest of the players were made into lines that would take turns skating after the guys who are going to play. For some dumb reason, and it was an oversight on my part, I didn't put Vic Hadfield on any line. I must be getting a little senile, because I did the same thing to Dale Tallon the other day. I didn't even realize what I had done when we started the line rushes. After a few minutes Fergie skated over to me and said: "Gee, what line do you want Hadfield to play on?" Now it struck me that I had overlooked Vic when I set up the lines. I didn't mean to. I told Fergie to tell Hadfield that I wanted him to spell off, or take turns with, the other left wingers who were not on a regular line. Hadfield was now standing by the boards and as Fergie went to talk to him I kept one eye on them. I could read Hadfield's expression from a distance and knew he was peeved.

They talked for a long time before Fergie skated back with the message. "He doesn't want to take part. He says he doesn't have to take this crap." As Fergie talked I watched Hadfield to see if he had changed his mind and was going to join in. Instead he left the ice and went to the bench, where he sat down and started reading the paper. He looked ridiculous sitting there reading the paper while all the other guys were out on the ice busting their humps. I went right over to him.

"I think you should be out there practicing. Your sitting there like that seems kind of silly."

"I'm not going to," Hadfield answered.

"Then you might as well take your stuff off," I told him. "There's no point in you just sitting here and making all of us look foolish."

"Why did you bring me here?" Hadfield asked.

"Like everyone else, I brought you to play hockey. Like everyone else, Vic, the players decide who plays on this team."

He misunderstood me because he looked kind of puzzled, and asked, "You mean the players voted, or something?"

"No. I mean a player determines who plays by the way he plays."

We weren't yelling at each other or really even arguing. There wasn't any anger visible in either of us. Without hurting Hadfield's feelings I was trying to let him know that, to this point, he just wasn't playing well enough to make the squad that dressed for the games.

As it turned out, these were my last words with Vic Hadfield. I wasn't going to beg him to come back onto the ice. I had invited him back, but I wasn't about to beg to get him to do it. I went back out to take charge of practice, which Fergie had taken over while I was with Hadfield.

A few minutes later, Al Eagleson was at the side of the rink, waving me over to talk to him. "I just talked to Hadfield and he's going home."

"Fine," I told Al, "get him on the first plane out of here. Get Mike Cannon to get him a ticket as quickly as possible." I thought for a moment about talking to him again. But then I said the hell with it. I didn't beg him to join this team. I wouldn't try to persuade him to stay.

At first I was disturbed. Then I thought "Good. If that's the way he feels, we've got to make sure he gets out of here before he has other guys feeling the same way." I heard this evening that he spoke to Dennis Hull about leaving, but as far as I know Dennis is still here. The strange part of it is that after Vic told Eagleson he was leaving, he joined in the rest of the practice. He even participated at the end when we did our tough skating drills. I thought that he had had a change of heart and was going to stay.

While we were on the ice, the players knew something was up but they weren't sure what. They saw Fergie and I talking to Hadfield, but except for a few of his Ranger teammates, I don't think the others realized he was leaving until the practice was over.

Then the word got around and I heard from our second defector, Rich Martin. Martin came up to me after practice and gave me this line: "I think I'd be better off back with Buffalo. I'm not going to play here. I'm not getting in shape and I want to get back to the Sabres' training camp. I want you to know there are no hard feelings."

"We'll have you on the first plane out of here," was all I told him.

I don't think this was planned between Martin and Hadfield. The word about Hadfield buzzed around and when Martin heard that someone was leaving, he wanted out too. It was fine with me, really. I don't have time for quitters. Everyone who doesn't want to be part of the team should be out of here. The worst thing a coach can do is keep trouble on his team. And right now these guys are a potentially fatal disease which could spread through the whole squad if I let them stay around.

The same goes for Josh Guivremont. On the bus back to the hotel, Fergie told me Guivremont also wanted to go home. I told Fergie that I wasn't going to do anything until Guivremont saw me himself. He came and saw me at the hotel. He said he felt that, like Martin, he wanted to get back with his team. He claimed he was worried he might not be able to make it with Vancouver unless he had a good camp.

I told Guivremont what I had told Martin: "I'd be happy if you get out of here as quickly as you can."

About this time Eagleson was talking to Martin about staying. Al came to me and said Martin was thinking about hanging around for two games to see if he would play or not. I told Al: "Unless he's with us all the way I don't want him around here. The same goes for Hadfield and Guivremont."

As far as I am concerned, the less I see of these guys, the better. Hadfield still has never told me personally he was leaving. He told Eagleson and I don't plan on carrying his bags to the airport for him. Martin and Guivremont are just as bad. This nonsense about getting back to their teams to get in shape is a joke. They've been practicing twice as long as any player back in Canada and will be in twice the shape of any guy on their team when they get back. The real reason they are leaving is that they know they're not going to be in the lineup and Moscow isn't as nice as Sweden if you're not playing. These players just can't see any sun on the horizon. They want to get out before they become a part of the downfall of hockey in Canada, and the "not being in shape" alibi is simply a cop out. What else can they say? They aren't man enough to stand up and say they wanted out on the moral commitment they made to Team Canada because things looked gloomy.

Actually, the more I look back on what has happened the more I feel these guys, particularly Martin and Hadfield, set us up for this. The other day in Stockholm I mentioned to Fergie that it appeared from some of the comments these guys were making to writers that they were protecting themselves in case we lost. If things didn't turn out the way they wanted, they could always say, "I told you so." Hadfield started it way back in Toronto when he talked about quitting before the Winnipeg game. I'd like to make them walk back to Canada myself. What really frosts me is that we have to come up with something like $3000 in cash to get them out of here in the morning. Fergie and Eagleson are going to have to take the money out of their own pockets to do it. The Russians don't believe in credit cards.

But I don't care if it costs $10,000. I want them out of here.

Moscow, Sept. 22

We're just not destined to win this thing. No matter what we do, these people beat us. Twice we had three-goal leads on them, and they came back to beat us, 5 to 4.

I'm still trembling. I guess it's anger wanting to escape from me. I've never felt so helpless in my life as I did tonight in the third period when the Russians scored five goals on us. Five goals against the "greatest" players in the world! Christ, that's still hard to believe, even though I saw it all happen just a couple of hours ago.

I've seen games turn around in a hurry before, but not like this one. After a slow start, we took control of the game and had them on the run at the end of the second period. Then the bottom fell out and I honestly don't know why. The Russians weren't any different from the first two periods. It was us. We stopped skating. But why? Why the hell do 17 of 18 guys all of a sudden stop skating? I could see it happening to one guy, or even a line. But a whole team? Explain it logically to me so that the next time it happens I'll know how to handle it.

I really expected to win this one. Despite our poor performance in Sweden last weekend, I had a good feeling about this game. Everything seemed to be shaping up better. At our noon meeting, following a light skate at the rink, I could sense the guys were fired up. When I was going over the game plan for tonight they were alert and bright. They were paying attention and not looking around. Everything we said seemed to be sinking in. Aside from the strategy to be employed, we also talked about our added incentive. I told them that the only thing that really counts is winning. That if we won this game, and went on to win the series, we would vindicate ourselves and all that we stand for.

We all went back to the hotel in the afternoon for our pregame meal and a nap. I couldn't sleep. Neither could Fergie. Our bus was set to leave for the arena at six, but when I got downstairs at 5:45, everyone was ready to go. We had a quiet ride out to the rink except for Pete Mahovlich yelling "Let's get ready" once in a while.

We were ready. There was no doubt in my mind. This thought was confirmed when we got to the dressing room and Phil Esposito started grumbling. When Phil's bitchy, he's ready. Phil is very meticulous and superstitious about his game preparation. Most guys want to get to the rink late, with just

Game Five, Moscow, September 22. In all the Moscow games the Canadian team was lifted by the loud support of the 3,000 fans who had made the trip to cheer them on. The cheering section got a lot of help from the players who weren't on the ice. (Photo by the Toronto Star)

Peter Mahovlich and Yvan Cournoyer on the attack for Canada. (Photo by the Toronto Star)

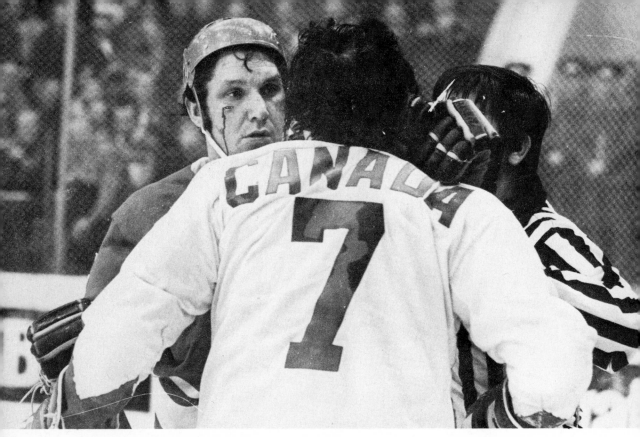

Game Six, Moscow, September 24. Tempers were high as the series neared a climax and Esposito and Ragulin, the veteran Russian defenseman, got into an argument. (Photo by the Toronto Star)

A close call for Dryden. . (Photo by the Toronto Star)

Game Seven, Moscow, September 26. Dragged down by Vasiliev, Paul Henderson somehow manages to get his shot away past Tretiak's shoulder into the net. It's the winner, bringing Canada level with the Soviet team, three games each. (Photo by the Toronto Star)

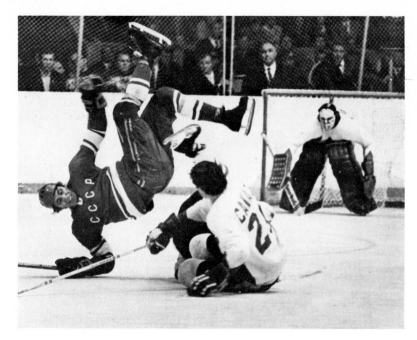

Game Eight, Moscow, September 28. The Russian top scorer, Yakushev, tries to go between two Canadian defensemen and has to do it the hard way. (Photo by the Toronto Star)

Defenseman Bill White appears out of nowhere to tip in a goal as the Canadians fight back. (Photo by the Toronto Star)

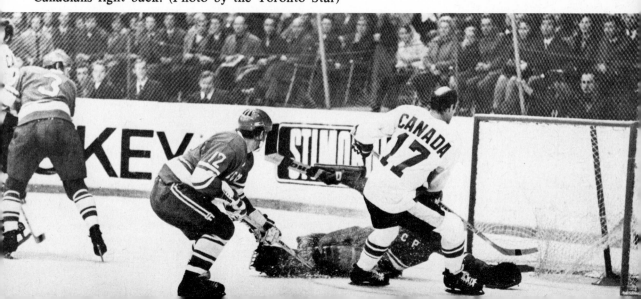

The faces say it all. Paul Henderson wins the series for Canada with a goal 34 seconds from the end. (Photo by the Toronto Star)

Back home in Canada, the whole country closed down as an estimated 16 million Canadians watched the final game. The Sparks Street Mall in Ottawa was as good a place as any to watch it. (Photo by C.P.)

When the game ended in a dramatic last-minute win for Canada, the entire country went a little crazy. Incidents like this, where celebrating kids halt traffic near Parliament Hill, happened in towns across the country. (Photo by C.P.)

When the team arrived back in Montreal they were greeted by Prime Minister Trudeau. Here the Prime Minister congratulates Bob Haggert, Alan Eagleson, and Harry Sinden. (Photo by the Montreal Gazette)

To the delight of Montreal fans the team toured the airport in two firetrucks, acknowledging their warm welcome. (Photo by the Montreal Gazette)

Serge Savard found it was a time when nobody minded a little horseplay—much. (Photo by the Montreal Gazette)

More than 80,000 fans braved the downpour to greet their heroes at Nathan Phillips Square in Toronto. (Photo by C.P.)

Harry Sinden addresses the huge crowd. (Photo by the Toronto Star)

Local and national hero Paul Henderson carried by Alan Eagleson and Tony Esposito at the Toronto civic reception. (Photo by C.P.)

Paul Henderson three days earlier, after the final game. It wasn't easy. (Photo by the Toronto Star)

enough time to get their equipment on and play the game. They don't like hanging around in the room. Phil is different. He goes at it like a bride preparing for her wedding. He puts his gloves and stick in front of him and they're not to be moved. He also makes sure that his sticks are crossed, for some reason. And when he puts on his equipment everything has to go on in sequence, always following the same pattern.

On this team we've also got three guys—Esposito, Pete Mahovlich, and Gary Bergman—who are superstitious about being the last man out of the dressing room. On their own teams, each has this role. Here, they've worked it out somehow that Bergman will be last. Maybe he has some seniority built up from the NHL.

This good feeling I had seemed to grow stronger as we got closer to the face-off. The players were just as keyed up as they were for the first game in Montreal. And they got a tremendous boost when they went out on the ice to warm up to a deafening ovation from the 3000 Canadian fans who came early to the game. If nothing else was gained tonight, we found we had at least 3000 Canadian comrades. They even cheered us in defeat, which was something. I'm as close to these guys as anyone, and I like them personally, but I couldn't be man enough to cheer after a game like that.

Ten minutes before we went out on the ice for the pre-game ceremonies, I brought the team into our large coaches' office. I knew they wouldn't need any Knute Rockne speeches. I just told them that their bodies and emotions were ready. All they had to do now to win was use their good hockey sense. I didn't want them falling into the same trap that snared us in Montreal, when we ran all over the place without thinking.

The Russians put on a first class show before the game. First, they presented our game captain, Ratelle, with the traditional gift of Soviet friendship, bread and salt. Big Jean won the hearts of the crowd when he reached down and kissed the girl who made the presentation. It was completely unexpected, but the Russians loved it.

Then we had a terrifically funny scene. Forty little girls, all about 12, came out and gave a bouquet of flowers to each player. Later, when the individual introductions were being made, Phil Esposito slipped on a petal or a stem and fell flat on his back in the middle of the ice. Phil, known in the NHL as a great actor anyway, now had center stage. Most guys would have scrambled to their feet in embarrassment, but not him. He stayed down in a sitting position for a few seconds, to the roar of the crowd and the smiles of the Russian players. (It's the first time I've seen them smile.) Then Phil rose rather majestically and gave a sweeping bow all around. Of course, our players enjoyed calling Phil a big ham and accused him of falling down on purpose for a few extra seconds on TV around the world.

The Russians carried the play in the early game, but just about midway through the period Perreault made a terrific rush, beating their big defenseman Lutchenko, whom we hadn't been able to beat at all in Canada. Then Perreault moved in and slipped the puck to Parise for our first goal.

After this we really began to assert ourselves. In the second period Bobby Clarke walked out from behind the net and stuck one between Tretiak's pads. Later, Henderson let fly with one of those quick shots of his and we were in front 3 to 0. Tony Esposito was terrific in goal for us throughout the first two periods.

Late in the second period Henderson was tripped going in on the Russian net and slid hard into the boards. He was dazed and had to be helped off the ice. Between periods I asked him if he would be ready for the third period, and he said he wanted to play.

I left Paul and got together with Fergie in the coaches' room to map out what we wanted to do in the third period. In the midst of our conversation Dr. Murray came in and said that Henderson wasn't going to play in the third period. I told him that Henderson said he wanted to play, and that if he wanted to play, he could.

Before going on the ice for the third period, we brought the team together again in the coaches' room. "We've got a three goal lead and the worst thing we can do is sit back and protect it", I said. "Let's go after them in their end. Forecheck them. Don't get caught in a box or a protective shell in our own end. If we do that, they'll murder us. Their team can score in bunches, but so can we. Let's go out there and score more goals. We've just played our best period since Toronto. And you can see that they're starting to falter. They're not as sharp as they were before this."

There was a lot of enthusiasm as we came back out for the

last period. The guys were hollering and ready to go. But about three minutes into the period, the Russians scored, because we were doing nothing except standing around. I started to get worried but the gutsy Henderson came right back with a goal for us and we had our three goal spread again, 4 to 1, with 15 minutes to play. The next few minutes, we played well, controlling the puck more than they did and having better chances.

Then suddenly, like someone put a curse on us, we fell apart. Maybe Frank Mahovlich is right when he calls these Russians "devils." They sure as hell have some kind of a spell on us. Right around the 9:00 mark they scored two goals in just eight seconds—not cheapies either. The Russians don't seem to score bad goals, because they never take desperation shots. When they pulled to within one goal so quickly, I looked at the bench and saw our guys had a quick downer. I raced up and down behind them yelling, "We're still going to win it. Let's get out there and skate. Get some goals."

They responded verbally, but not physically. I don't think I ever saw a good team like ours so completely outplayed as we were in the next five minutes. We couldn't keep up with them. They were flying by us, beating us to every loose puck, and forcing us into every imaginable mistake. I knew it was just a matter of time. And I was right. They got two goals in the next five minutes and took a 5 to 4 lead.

What hurts is that the winning goal was just as much my fault as anyone else's. One strategic change we made for this game was to have our defensemen gamble at the Russian blue line more than they did in Canada. We told them to hang in there a little longer and take a chance at a loose puck in the Russian end if they got the opportunity. Whitey Stapleton, following my instructions, tried to do this. He lost the race to the puck and when he tried to recover, he fell. This sent the Russians out of their zone two-on-one. At the blue line they sent their man—Vikulov, I guess—in free on Tony for the winning goal.

Normally, the Soviet crowd is very quiet and subdued. They like to treat hockey in the same fashion as ballet, the type of event you watch quietly, without emotion. From the beginning and throughout the game our supporters had kept up a constant "Go, go Canada!" chant. In response, the Russians started chanting something like "Shiboo," which, I understand, means "get the puck." When the Soviets took the lead the building exploded. It was bedlam, not really like the Russians.

Maybe the noise woke us up. We played well in the final minutes and had a couple of good chances. None would go in the net and as the clock counted down I knew I didn't have control of myself. I went right to the dressing room and closed the door behind me in the office. I didn't want to see the players. I didn't want to see anyone but Fergie. I needed someone to share my agony. The Russians had set some coffee on my desk in demitasse cups. I picked one up, took a sip, and then shattered it against the wall, splattering the cup, saucer, and coffee all over the room, myself, and Fergie. We were both so frustrated we didn't even mind. We must have felt it was penance for being losers.

We stayed in the room, stalking up and down, cursing out loud until we were sure all the players had left. I didn't want to see any players. I would have said the wrong thing. There wasn't any right thing to say after this. I've said all I could for six weeks. They've listened to me enough. Now they've got to come up with their own answers.

6
Game Six

Moscow, Sept. 23

If we pass this way again, give me a kick in the butt if I'm stupid enough to pick 21-year-old kids to a team like this. There might be all kinds of positive arguments to lower the voting age, and the drinking age, to 18, but you could never prove it by me. Not today anyway.

We had our fourth defector today, Gilles Perreault. Like Martin and Guivremont, his buddies, he is just a kid and very immature. When I had the team on the ice for practice this morning, Perreault came to me and said he wanted to leave. He gave me the same party line as Martin and Guivremont: he had to get back to his own team; he wasn't in shape. His excuse, like that of the other two, was not true.

I'm even more bothered by Perreault than the other two. At least he has played some in this series. Last night he set up our first goal. But the truth is he didn't think he played enough. I had him dressed as a spare forward, mostly to spell off Phil Esposito after Phil would take a long shift where he might be forced to stay on the ice as a penalty killer, or on the power play.

After last night's first period, I watched Perreault closely, figuring he might be in for a big game. He's a fine skater and should be much better on this bigger ice surface. Yet, in the second period he had nothing. His legs seemed to be gone. Every time I put him on the ice he got caught up ice and made it easy for the Soviets to start attacking. I made up my mind that Perreault wasn't going to play in the third period because he's a poor defensive player to start with and we didn't want the Russians to score any easy goals. Not playing in the third period hurt his feelings. This is the reaction of a kid, a baby. When things don't go your way, go in the corner and sulk. Or, in the case of these three, go back to your team where you'll be the star and everyone can fawn over you and make you feel wanted. When he told me he was leaving, Perreault asked me not to make him look bad with the press. My reaction was: "Don't worry. I'll have you out of here as fast as possible. There's a flight leaving soon and you'll be on it."

Although I'll never accept the way they quit on us, it was my error in the first place bringing them on the squad. I should have known enough to check out how mature they were. We've got other kids here that age, like Marcel Dionne and Dale Tallon, and they're hanging in with us. Sure, they're not happy, and I don't expect them to be. No hockey player worth his salt is happy about not playing. But these kids have the right attitude. Tallon told me the other day, right in front of Martin and Perreault, "I feel lucky I was chosen to this team. Someday I hope I'm good enough to play regularly in a series like this."

Martin was our very last left wing and wouldn't have been picked to the squad in the first place. He was my replacement when they wouldn't let Bobby Hull play. Guivremont was a political choice. When we got down to our last defensive spot we had a list of 10 to 15 guys who were all about the same. We took Guivremont because we were going to play one game in Vancouver and we had only one player from out that way on the squad, Tallon. Next time there won't be any political or geographical choices. Next time, character will mean as much as ability.

The players laughed off Perreault's defection. All the money we made in the exhibition games on this tour is going into a pot to be divided at the end of the tour. When we were coming back to the hotel on the bus after practice today Eddie

Johnston voiced the opinion for all to hear: "Does anyone else want to go home? If we can get rid of a few more the pot will get bigger for the rest of us."

We had a good workout today. It was the first time I talked to the players since the nightmare of last night. I got them together at center ice and told them the game was gone and there wasn't any way we could get it back. "We have to turn our thoughts ahead to tomorrow night, and not look back," I told them. "We played darn well most of the game. If we sustained it for three periods we would have beaten them. If we play that way for three periods tomorrow night we will beat them. And that's what's going to happen."

I really believe that our training in the NHL is going to help us. As pros, we're used to losing tough games and bouncing back the next night. With 78 games a year to play, you can't go around feeling sorry for yourself every time you lose. These guys, many of them, have lost heartbreakers in the Stanley Cup playoffs and then had to lift themselves up for a game the next night.

As our practice went along, they worked briskly and seemed to have dismissed the loss. For this practice, Fergie and I devised a new drill. After reviewing the game, it dawned on us that we could control the game any time we were able to have good puck control in the Soviet end. The only weak link we can find in the Russians' play is their poor defensive work once the other team has the puck under control in the Soviet zone. We never tried it before, but today we had five players rushing against three defenders for an hour, with the attackers trying to hold the puck as long as they could in the offensive zone, making as many passes as possible, before giving it up. We feel this will help us to be more stable on offense, and put pressure on the Russians at the same time.

I have three people I'm concerned with—the two German referees, and Ken Dryden. We each named a referee for the first game. I picked the Swede, Dahlberg. They took the Czech, Bata. By international standards they did a good job. By NHL standards they didn't. I'd much rather have them going again tomorrow night than the Germans under any standards. There's no choice at this point. We have to live with the Germans.

Dryden is going to be in goal. He didn't play well in either start he had at home, and we didn't get a chance to play him in

Sweden. That might prove to have been a mistake. We used Esposito in the first Sweden game because he was our choice for the first game here. And we used Johnston in the second game because he hadn't had any work at all, and we didn't want him coming in here in an emergency with no previous game experience. I think Dryden will get his game together.

The referees? I don't think I'm going to sleep too well with them on my mind.

Moscow, Sept. 24

The spell is wearing off.

Whatever they've had going for them isn't there anymore. We eliminated a big part of the Russian mystique tonight when we beat them 3 to 2, despite those two West German stiffs who call themselves referees. One thing about these guys, they're consistent—always bad. That wasn't any fluke in Sweden. Tonight these guys strengthened my belief that they are the most incompetent officials I've ever seen.

It was a great win for us. We're still a game down in this series—they've got three wins, we've got two and there's one tie. But we're in good shape, believe me. The Russians are faltering. I thought I spotted it in the last game, but they came back to beat us and I thought I must have been imagining things. We're coming on and getting better each game, forcing them into mistakes. They're not as smooth passing the puck as they were in Canada. And Tretiak is starting to come apart a little. He was sleeping on the winning goal tonight and for us he took the nap at the best possible time.

Another great thing about this victory is that we won't have to look at those Germans again. They're gone. For the last two games we've got the Swede and the Czech. We're lucky. If the Germans had one of the last two games it would be just impossible to win the series. They did everything they could to help the Russians in this game right to the very end. I'm not saying the Russians have bought them off or anything like that, but surer than hell they aren't being fair. Any fool can see they are looking for us. We had eight penalties for a total of 31 minutes; the Russians got two minors.

Near the end of the game, when we were battling to hold the lead, the refs really gave us the shaft. With two minutes left they called a really cheap penalty on Ellis. They were trying to do everything in their power to bail out the Soviets. A referee never gives a penalty in the last two minutes unless it's a flagrant violation. This wasn't even close to being flagrant. We weren't going to let this game get away. Our players would have eaten the puck at the end if they had to.

I've seen Phil Esposito play a lot of hockey games but this is the first time I'd ever seen him block shots. The other guys we had out there—Stapleton, White, Mahovlich—were also throwing their bodies in front of the puck to frustrate the Russians. And we did.

I was happy with the changes I made. Coming out of Sweden, Fergie and I decided we would try to play the same guys every game here and go with a set line-up. The first game changed our mind. We put Serge Savard back in and took out Seiling. Seiling didn't like it and told Fergie he thought we were blaming him for the 5 to 4 loss Friday night. That wasn't the reason at all. Park and Bergman and White and Stapleton had been our best two defensive pairs. We wanted to get Savard back into the line-up, so we paired him with Lapointe, a teammate of his in Montreal. We felt Savard would work better with Lapointe and we were right. Frank Mahovlich also sat down. Frank, who played poorly in the first Moscow game, hasn't had a real good one since Toronto. With Frank out, I moved Cournoyer up to play on a line with Esposito and Parise. This meant I had to find a left wing to play with the center and right wing I had left, Ratelle and Gilbert. Guess who would have been it if he were still here: Hadfield. Instead I went with Dennis Hull, and what a break!

The first period was scoreless but well played by both teams. We were flying up and down the ice. It was as exciting as you could get without any goals. Dryden played well. He had his confidence.

Early in the second period the Soviets took the lead. Their defenseman, Liapkin, let one go from the point. I think Dryden should have had it but he misjudged the shot. It was lower than he thought and went in under his glove. (I didn't learn until later that Dryden had changed his style. The Russians had put so many goals behind him in the two games he worked before this that he decided to sit back further in the net, rather than come out to cut down the angles. When he stayed back on this one, he gave Liapkin more of the net to shoot at.)

About four minutes later, our additions broke it open. First Hull came across the crease and lifted one over Tretiak. Then Berenson, filling in for Perreault, set up Cournoyer in front, and just 15 seconds later we were ahead 2 to 1. We were buzzing. The Russians were staggering around trying to recover when Henderson intercepted a pass in the Russian zone, out near the blue line, took two strides toward the net, and bombed a 30-footer at Tretiak. It went right between his pads. He seemed stunned. He didn't expect Henderson to shoot. This was the first time in the series the Soviet goalie didn't seem alert. He does have some flaws.

We made the lead stand up this time, despite the officiating, which was really bad. After two periods we had played 15 minutes shorthanded. The calls were so obviously malicious our bench was going crazy. Fergie and I were yelling so much some of the players thought we had lost our minds. I remember Berenson telling me once to calm down. I just looked at him. Another time Dryden skated over and looked at me like I was nuts. I told one of the other players, "Get that damn Dryden back in the net!"

Fergie and I knew what we were doing. There's only one way to stop a referee in a situation like that—embarrass him. Hold him up to ridicule before the crowd, and the world in this case, with the game on TV throughout Europe and North America. We wanted to make sure their countrymen watching in Germany knew what jerks they were. This is why we made a scene. We threw towels on the ice and kept raging at them. Finally, they gave Fergie a bench penalty and he wanted to clobber them. Fergie didn't do anything that bad, he just called one of them kraut, or something.

From this point on I became a little scared. The players— the ones on the ice and the ones in street clothes behind the bench—were so incensed I was afraid that if they ever got close to these officials they'd kill them. We came out of the second period leading 3 to 2, and all of us raced after the officials who were going toward their dressing room. Bobby Orr and I got there first. We chased them up the runway screaming. We shouldn't have been behaving this way but they didn't leave us any choice. If they were going to do a job on us, we weren't going to let them off the hook. Just before they got to the dressing room one of them stopped in his tracks to answer us. Orr was right on his heels, and when the referee—

Baader—stopped, Bobby ran into him. Bobby gave him a shove, and faster than you could yell "cop," the Soviet police and officials were all around us. We looked like clowns once again, but at this point we were beyond caring. We're not going to sit around and take the shaft any more.

In the dressing room I could sense everyone was uptight about the officials. I talked to them a long time about the referees and pointed out that this was our last chance. We had to win. "We're frustrated, but we have to have poise to play this last period. Let's get our senses back," I told them.

Now I did something I've never done before as a coach. I purposely kept the team in the dressing room longer than I was supposed to. This could be our last act and we were going to play it our way. I called for Stan Mikita, who was in street clothes, to go out and inspect the ice surface. Before the third period of our last game here the Russians put too much water on the ice. Stan checked and told me they did the same thing this time. Great. We had the excuse: we would sit in the room until the ice set properly. The Russians were on the ice and so were the officials. But I kept our squad in the room until I was positive everyone was calmed down and ready to give his top effort the next 20 minutes.

When we came out, we discovered we had psyched them out. The Russians and the officials had wondered what we were doing in the room so long. They didn't know what to make of it. The last period was beautiful. It was the first time in the series we finished stronger than they did.

In our tantrum following the first game here, Fergie and I had refused to go to the press conference the Russians had set up. We got nailed for this by the press. Tonight, for some reason, we went gladly. However, Bobrov didn't show. I guess we're not the only poor sports around here.

The Soviet writers asked how I could act in such a manner toward the officials who, in Europe, are held sacred. I wanted to answer, "If they're so goddamn sacred, what the hell was your Mr. Sterevoitov doing kicking chairs around and threatening them in Toronto?"

But I didn't. It wasn't the time or place for that. I just wanted, in other ways, to tell them that the Germans were completely incompetent and would not work this series again. I added, "Tomorrow we will meet with the Soviet officials to make sure this is the case." When I got back to the hotel tonight I took Eagleson aside and told him to arrange the meeting. I would make sure that these guys didn't work another game of this series.

7
Game Seven

Moscow, Sept. 25.

We got the big monkey off our backs today. The Germans are definitely finished in this series. I had a sneaking suspicion the Russians would go back on our deal, but I have to give them credit. They surprised me, and agreed to let the Swede and the Czech work the last two games.

However, today was the first time I noticed some bitterness developing. I guess it really started last night when Eagleson had some trouble in the stands with one of the Russian players who didn't dress for the game. He was sitting near Mrs. Kryczka, wife of Joe Kryczka, the chairman of the Canadian Amateur Hockey Association. In the first period Mrs. Kryczka tapped the man in front of her on the shoulder and asked him to stop jumping up and down in front of her. The man, who turned out to be a Russian player (I don't know which one), put his fist up to Mrs. Kryczka. Eagleson spotted this, and when he moved in to make his presence felt, some of their secret police tried to run him out of the arena.

(The KGB is all over the place. During the games you can see one positioned in almost every aisle of the arena. We know

99

we are being followed constantly. I don't mind that, but I do mind the way they operate. They get physical with people, and they don't ask any questions first. And they don't care if you're Canadian or Russian. If you're doing something they don't like, they just come up and grab you, and shove you around until you get the message.)

I neglected to mention something that happened after the third period last night. When we headed for the dressing room, the entire promenade around the stadium was wall to wall with the Red Army. After our jam in the runway with the officials, they called out the "militia," which is how they refer to the army. When I got to our dressing room, they were lined up shoulder to shoulder in the runway. They tried to keep me and the players in street clothes out of the dressing room, pretending they didn't know who we were. We finally had to shove our way through, just about the time one of their officials came to identify us for the soldiers. When we came out of the arena later, we saw them all getting back on trucks to drive back to their base.

This morning at the rink we could feel more waves of resentment from them. From earlier arrangements, we were scheduled to have the ice from 10:30 to 12:30. At noon, Bobrov came down to the ice and told me through an interpreter to get off the ice. I told him to: "Drop dead."

When the interpreter relayed the message, Bobrov was stunned. Then I pulled out the itinerary which showed we had the ice until 12:30, and the Russians had it for the next two hours. Bobrov still didn't want to accept this so I told him: "I don't care what you say. We're not leaving until 12:30. If you want to bring your players out on the ice before that, I don't know what might happen to them." He thought for a second and agreed we would have the ice for another 30 minutes.

Leaving the ice I spotted Alex Gresko, who we feel is the number one Russian we have dealt with. I didn't know the man with him. I had first seen the other man last night in the runway when we had the joust with the officials. When I got into our coaches room I asked Bob Haggert to go out and bring Gresko in for our meeting. Gresko brought the other man, a Mr. Romansky, chairman of the committee on sports and physical education.

Romansky does not speak English. Gresko does. I thought they wanted to talk about the officials like I did, but they had other things in mind. In quick order they admonished us for the night before. Romansky did most of the talking through Gresko as his interpreter. He went into a 15-minute sermon in which he lodged three official protests against our conduct the night before. First, he was upset by the way the Canadians acted toward the officials. Second, he was bothered by the way our players in street clothes were acting at the games. Third, they complained about the behaviour of Gary Bergman. Although I didn't know it, Gary had been needling coach Bobrov when he skated by the Soviet bench. He didn't swear or anything, he was just being sarcastic.

"Coaches and officials are sacred in Russia," Romansky said. "If your players address our coach in this manner again we may not be able to control our players." We let them get it all off their chests, because we really didn't give a damn. When they were finished I told them: "Look. None of this would have happened if you hadn't picked those West Germans to work in this series. They are totally incompetent. We had a bad time with them in Sweden and when they worked such a poor game here again last night, our players became incensed. If you guarantee me that the Germans won't officiate again in this series, then I will promise you there will be no further trouble from any Canadian player or official."

They nodded, and told us they agreed. The West Germans will not work again. I could feel the relief pouring out of me. But I also wanted to get in a dig at the Russian players. "Your players," I told them, "do things during a game which we consider underhanded by our standards. This prompts our players to respond in a way that might be strange to European fans. Your players have to share the blame for the times the games have become rough."

They didn't say anything, but I could tell they didn't believe this at all. Instead Romansky came back at us about Bobby Orr, whom Romansky had seen push the referee the night before. "I have great respect for Orr, but you should teach your players to control their tempers," said Romansky. Throughout our dealings with the Russians, Gresko had been the mediator. When Romansky continued the conversation about our players, Gresko hung his head. He didn't like this controversy. But the meeting ended on a friendly note, with all of us reviewing what had been agreed upon.

I was pleased today with the way the people back home are

getting behind us. We're being flooded with telegrams and messages. The guys are pasting them up on the walls near our dressing room at the arena.

I'm becoming superstitious for the first time in my life. I ran today's practice identically to the one we had the other day. Before last night's game I remembered that the only time in this series I didn't watch our team warm up was in Toronto, and we won. Last night I didn't watch the warmup, and we won again. I'm not watching warmup anymore. I'm also superstitious about this pair of alligator shoes I have. They've been with me for our two victories. I know it's nonsense, but I'm afraid to change.

Moscow, Sept. 26

It's all even now. Even in number of victories, even in number of games stolen.

I still consider they stole that game from us Sunday night with five goals in the final period. But we stole one back tonight on an incredible goal by Paul Henderson in the final few minutes. We beat them 4 to 3 after they had outplayed us.

Our defensive play saved us. Offensively, we stunk. We couldn't attack as a team at all. Our goals were almost all great individual efforts, and Henderson's was as good as you're ever going to see. It was the most exciting goal I've ever seen. It freaked out the players, too, they went wild. I've never seen a team react to a goal the way our players did tonight. The score was tied 3 to 3 with just over two minutes left to play. Make that exactly 2:06 to play because the first thing I did after I stopped kissing and hugging everyone was to look at the clock.

Up to this point I was praying for a tie. We were out of it. They had the puck almost all the time. I thought for sure they were going to put one in and then bury us, like they did at the end of the first game in Montreal. We hung on though, and Henderson got another big one. Savard set it up for him with a good pass. Serge had the puck along the right boards in our end when he moved around a Russian and hit Henderson on the fly going into center ice. Both teams were one man short, and Savard's pass let Henderson get up the middle before the two Russian wings could back check. He still had the two Russian defensemen in front of him and as he came across the Soviet blue line he made a move to go through the middle. As he did, he lost control of the puck and it rolled ahead of him. When the two Russians saw that Henderson was going for the middle, they closed in to take him down. As they did, the puck bounced off one of their skates and rolled behind them to Henderson's left. Paul is fast and he swept around the Russians to the left, got the puck back, and moved in on Tretiak from the left side.

Since he's a righthand shot, Henderson wanted to cut in front of the goal so he could shoot with his forehand. As he closed in, one of the Russians recovered and started to knock him down. Paul let the puck go at this instant and rifled it past Tretiak's right elbow into the net. We exploded on the bench, but then Fergie noticed that the red light didn't go on behind the net. "Get onto the ice, get out there with Henderson!" Fergie starting yelling at our players. We started shoving them all over the boards. Fergie realized they might think about robbing us out of the goal. We sent the players out for the big celebration to make sure they didn't try to take it away from us. Finally, the light went on, but for only a tenth of a second.

It took us a few minutes to get the players back on the bench and calmed down. We still had to play the final two minutes and the Russians can score like lightning. They had scored twice in eight seconds, and another time in 21 seconds. We knew they didn't need two minutes to get back to a tie. But we held them off and now all we have to do is beat them Thursday night.

I told the press after the game, "I think the last game will be the greatest ever in hockey." I meant it. The talent is here. The emotion is here. The drama is here. And both teams are getting their share of luck. We got ours tonight, so maybe this superstition stuff is working. I did all the same things tonight. I've got Fergie pulling with me, the same as the other day. We met at 5:15 in my room and had two scotch and waters while we went over our plans; we had two 'pops' before we won Sunday.

We made one major move today that turned out to be important. The Russians, in the last two games, have been all over Phil Esposito, and he hasn't scored. They've put number 16, Petrov, on his back. We decided to get them away from that by skating four lines. We knew they wouldn't break up their team work to counteract this. To get four lines we benched Berenson and dressed Goldsworthy, who teamed with Peter Mahovlich as Phil's fourth line wings. Phil also skated his regular turn with the first line.

Peter Mahovlich is into this superstition thing, too. Tonight on the way to the rink he sat in the jump seat beside the bus driver where he had sat before the last game. As we got onto the bus, he made sure everyone had the exact same seat as last time.

Once the game started, the Russians swarmed all over us. They controlled the puck, but many times they waited too long to shoot. Our defense was sound, or else they might have had four or five goals more than they got. Phil got two goals in the first period, both out of the slot. That was all the pressure we put on Tretiak. The rest was on us. They also scored twice in the first period. The second period was scoreless.

We went ahead 3 to 2 early in the third on Gilbert's first goal of the series. It was a helluva move. Rod really hustled on the play, and ended up moving out from behind the Soviet goal to knock it past Tretiak.

Bergman went out a couple of minutes later on a penalty, and the Russians tied it on a beautiful power play. As much as I hated it at the time, I have to praise them. This was something out of a hockey textbook, as close to perfection as you can come on the power play. Maltsev had the puck in the right corner as they set up their five-man pattern. We were in our four man defensive box. Twice Maltsev faked a pass, both times with his head and body, back to his right pointman. After the second fake, almost without looking, he blistered a pass across the goal mouth to the other side, where Yakushev had snuck in behind Brad Park to stick the puck in the open side. Tony Esposito, great in goal for us the whole game, didn't have a chance. "I'm sorry," said Park when he came off the ice. "I knew he was there but the pass was so quick I didn't have time to cover."

The Soviets continued to press after this and only because one of their cheap shots caught up with them did we get back in the game. With about five minutes left, Mikhailov grabbed Bergman around the neck behind our net and tried to pull him to the ice. The puck was at their feet. Bergman got mad and belted him, and we had the first fight of the series.

Bergman dropped his stick and gloves. Mikhailov, instead of using his fists, started to kick. Five or six times he kicked Bergman with the toe of his skates. Our players were going berserk on the bench when they saw the Russian kicking. Bergman couldn't get at him because the officials were in between, but Cournoyer, who seldom fights in the NHL, got so mad he moved in and ripped five or six good left hooks at Mikhailov. If Bergman had ever got free, he would have killed him.

Mikhailov is the Russian smart aleck anyway. During the second period he had come over past our bench a few times and started sassing Fergie. He gave him the circular motion behind the head, meaning "You're soft." I should have let Fergie nail him right then and there, but I thought it would be more fun to lodge a protest. If Bergman can't needle Bobrov, what the hell right does this guy have bothering Fergie? I sent word at the end of the period about the incident, and Bobrov sent word back that it would not happen again.

Mikhailov had kicked Bergman so viciously in the fight that he ripped Gary's stockings, put holes in his shinpads where the point punctured them, and cut the side of his leg. You'd never know it by the officials. They gave them both five minutes for roughing and said they never saw Mikhailov kick.

The officials did a good job of calling penalties against us tonight. I'm serious. We got what we deserved. Overall, they were poor though. As they have done in every game of the series, they let the Russians get away with murder. Because of the double penalty to Bergman and Mikhailov, both sides had to play with four skaters in the final minutes. And this opened the door for Henderson, who appears to have Tretiak's number.

8
Game Eight

Moscow, Sept. 27

They lied to us. Now they're saying that the West Germans are going to referee the last game. Can you believe that? Spirit of friendship, my ass. These guys would steal the fillings out of your teeth if you smiled long enough. Well, they're not going to get away with it. They think they've got us hanging by our thumbs, but we're not going to take anything from them. We've got another meeting scheduled tomorrow to make the final decision on the referees. They insist it's going to be the West Germans, and they're playing the stubborn role.

I should have known something like this was going to happen. Last night before the seventh game, one of their top officials, a guy named Victor, came into the dressing room and said he would like to have a meeting to choose the officials for game eight. I told him, "Get the hell out of here. We've got an agreement and that's it. It's the Czech and the Swede, or nobody." He backed off, but said he'd see me after the game. I didn't see him after the game so I thought we wouldn't have any problems. At the post-game press conference, one of the reporters asked about the referees for the last game and I told him: "It's all set. An agreement was reached before the seventh game that the West Germans would not work the remainder of the series." All of the Russian officials were at the press conference and heard my answer. None of them said a thing.

Today they are singing a different tune. This morning Gary Smith from the Canadian Embassy came to me at the rink with the message that the Russians now wanted the West Germans. The Russians had contacted Smith to tell him that they—the Russians—had met with all of the referees at the Metropole Hotel, and discovered that the other referees did not want to discriminate against their colleagues. The referees themselves, as a collective group, wanted the West Germans to work so that no one would be discriminated against.

In the first place, the Russians had no right meeting secretly with the officials. In the second place, I didn't give a damn who felt discriminated against. Those Germans aren't going to be in that game. After practice I went back to the hotel where Gresko and Eagleson were meeting in Al's room. Gresko went into his big speech about the Russians—himself, Bobrov, Romansky and Kulagin—not wanting to discriminate against the Germans. We told him that Ferguson, Sinden, and Eagleson would not let their team play if the Russians went back on their word. Then I asked him: "Weren't you and Romansky the ones who gave us your word the other day that the two West Germans would not work again?" He said that he understood it that way, but that there must have been another meeting to change it back. Or else, Romansky lost something in the translation that day and didn't quite understand what was going on. We knew this was a crock of bull. These guys don't miss a trick. It was now apparent to us that they wanted the Germans going for them in this last game because they didn't want to lose the series. Until last night, they thought they were going to win without any problem. Now they're looking for insurance for the last game. When we couldn't get any further with Gresko in Eagleson's room, he phoned the arena where the Russian team was practicing and set up a meeting at the rink for three o'clock. We all went back out and for the next hour reviewed every agreement made from July to the last few days. In every one of them, we had the Russians cold and they knew it. But they wouldn't budge. Finally Eagleson told them: "If you try to use the West Germans we won't play the game." We didn't really mean it, and they acted like they knew we didn't mean it. Finally, it was suggested that it be settled at the embassy level. We hockey people couldn't seem to get it straightened out. We left it that way in the afternoon, but tonight at the Bolshoi Ballet, I met Arthur Lang, the top Canadian government official at the games. He told me the embassy was passing the buck back to us.

He also told me that he heard of our threat to pull out and he assured the Russians that we would play. That was really great! Here we are trying to bluff these people, and he's turning over our hole card. All of this has upset our players, and we have enough problems without all of this other nonsense. Today at practice I found three defensemen hurting. Bergman has a bad back. Stapleton has a bad ankle. And White's heel is sore. I expect all of them to play, but I won't know until tomorrow. We gave some thought to bringing Orr in for this last game, but soon dismissed the idea. His knee is still bad, and he's not in shape. I thought that instead of playing fulltime I might just use him on the power play, but we don't get any power plays from these officials. We've averaged about one a game. And I'm not going to dress a guy for two minutes' action. Right now I have only two changes for this big game. Dryden will be our goaltender. I went over to him during practice and told him "You're going to start". He said thanks and started to skate away when I added; "and finish too." I wanted him to know that we're going all the way with him. I don't want him to think that if he blows one early, we're liable to panic and yank him out. I'll get Frank Mahovlich back in there as well. Frank hasn't been playing well, which is why I benched him for the last two games. I'm bringing him back because he knows how to play a big game. He's had plenty of seventh game Stanley Cup action under his belt and the pressure shouldn't bother him. Right now, that experience in the big game is our biggest asset. The Russians have never been in big games like we have. I also told Dale Tallon to be ready. He'll warm up with us before the game and if either Bergman, Stapleton, or White can't make it, Tallon will take his place. I think the kid has what it takes to play a big game for us. On the way back to the hotel on the bus, the German referees were all the players could talk about. "We shouldn't take any guff from these people," said Orr. And the others backed him up. I felt badly about all of this because I had assured our players the Germans wouldn't be back.

I also felt bad for Gary Smith. He had one helluva day around here. Last night, after our victory, one of our supporters got tipsy and started moving some furniture around in the bar at the hotel. He also was playing his trumpet which doesn't go over too well with the KGB. They moved in on him and he nailed one of them with his trumpet. It turned out to be a sour note. They took the guy to the local jail, stripped him naked, made him stand in an ice cold shower for six straight hours, tattooed both his heels to show he was a prisoner of the Soviets, fined him $260, and sentenced him to 15 days hard labor to be followed by one to three years in prison. And they weren't just bluffing! If it wasn't for our government people here, that fan would be long gone. Instead, the Russians are going to keep him locked up until his plane is ready Saturday. Then they are personally going to escort him to the plane. These people are tough. But tomorrow they're going to find that we're just as tough.

Moscow, Sept. 28

This has to be what heaven feels like. If there's anything that can make a person feel better than I do right now, the man upstairs must be keeping it locked up in some special place. We beat the Russians today 6 to 5 in a fantastic hockey game. I've been wrong about a lot of things in this series, but I was right when I said it was going to be the greatest hockey game ever played. It was—if you're Canadian.

It's now early morning and I've had my fair share of champagne. But I could be on a bender for a week and still remember every detail of this bittersweet day. I'll remember the good things like Paul Henderson's courageous goal in the last 34 seconds to win it for us. I'll remember the bad things like the way the Russians broke their word and tried to put the screws to us with the officials. The name of the game is still to put the puck in the net and in the end we did it three times to beat them in the final period. In the end, they were leaning over their sticks and we were doing the celebrating. They've got no complaints. They had us where they wanted us— leading 5 to 3 going into the third period—and then we took it away from them. They had one of their stooges refereeing— Kompalla—and we still beat them even when it was obvious that he was going out of his way to do everything to aid their cause. We discovered first thing in the morning that they were intent on getting the two Germans into the game. We now know why. These Germans would do anything the Russians wanted them to do.

After our practice we met at the rink with Gresko and Romansky. The first 60 minutes was a repeat of the day before. We reviewed all the prior agreements which would have given us the right to pick the referees for this final game and they still refused to budge. Finally I jumped up and told Gresko rather heatedly: "Listen, we're going to play this hockey game with the Swede and the Czech or no way at all." Gresko looked at me coldly for a second, with a look that could kill if it were possible. "In Russia," he said, "we make the decisions, not you."

The implications here were not just for hockey. He was giving us the theme song for this system. In Russia when the big boys say jump—you say how high. But Eagleson, myself, and Fergie weren't buying it. "Okay then," I said. "I want you now to officially break your word. Tell me that we can't pick the officials for this game as we agreed last July." "You can't pick them," Gresko answered, "the Germans will be the officials." We all flew into a rage. Fergie jumped up and started calling them every name in the book. Al really blistered Gresko, because all along we thought he was the good guy on their side and he's turned out to be the biggest creep of the bunch. There were threats going back and forth on both sides when Gary Smith from our embassy, who was acting as an interpreter, told the Russians that they should consider our previous concession of picking one official each. The Russians huddled privately after this and in a few minutes came back and said yes, being the good sports that they were, they would agree to let us pick one official. This was fine with us because even though we ranted and raved that we were going to pull out, we had decided ahead of time that we would play this game even if we had to do it with the two West Germans on the ice. "We'll take the Swede," I told the Russians, who now informed us—"We're sorry, but the Swede is sick. We happened by his hotel this morning and he doesn't feel well enough to work tonight." This was the first idea we had that the Swede might not be available. Immediately, Fergie, Al, and myself caught each other's eye and knew the Russians were tampering with the officials even more than we thought. "We'll still take the Swede," we said. "But if he can't work, we'll take the Czech. Who is your pick?" "Kompalla," they answered. This stunned us for a moment. We thought they'd go for Baader because he was the worst. That's what our team had nicknamed these two guys—"Baader and Worst." After the meeting I got Joe Kryczka and told him to get down to the Metropole and check on the Swede.

This meeting with the Russians ended with hard feelings all around. We shook hands, but it was the cold fish treatment. We hustled back to the hotel because we had our whole Team Canada entourage waiting at a meeting which was called to let everyone know how to get out of here as quickly as possible and on our way to Czechoslovakia. After the meeting the players took their nap and then came down for the pre-game meal, where we encountered the case of the missing Canadian steaks. We should have had 100 steaks left for our pre-game meal but the Russians somehow misplaced them. They claim it was poor Canadian arithmetic. In this country four times 50 is 300. We thought it was 200. So the kitchen staff here at the Intourist Hotel will have a few steak dinners on us in the next few weeks. I hope they choke on it like their team did on the ice tonight. Because of our hassle with the Russians about the officials, we weren't able to hold our usual team meeting on the day of the game. Instead, we had it in the dressing room before the game, which meant leaving 15 minutes earlier. Fergie and I made sure everything was in proper order. I had my alligator shoes on. We had our two scotch and waters in my room at precisely 5:15, and when we got on the team bus we took the same seats. Cournoyer had been sitting in mine, but Pete Mahovlich made sure everyone was in the right place. On the way out Peter gave us his usual yell: "Are we ready?" Now everyone on the bus shouted back at him "Yes! Yes!" Then it became quiet again as we rode along, studying all the Russians walking home from work—all those blank, unsmiling faces. We were ready to keep their frowns in place. Inside our dressing room I called everyone together. They stood around my coaches' office half undressed and just stared silently as I went over the 'commandments' we had put together for the Russians—our game plan, so to speak. We had just finished when John Forristal, one of our trainers, came into the room his eyes dancing with excitement.

"I just saw Kharlamov coming into the rink and he's limping like hell. The only way they'll get that guy on the ice tonight is to give him a shot." Kharlamov, the Russian star, had been injured in the sixth game of the series, when his ankle jumped up and tried to assault Whitey Stapleton's hockey stick. He missed the last game, but the Russians were pulling out all the stops for this one. In minutes, word came back that Kharlamov was getting a shot of novocaine and would be on the ice. "I don't want any of you guys to go out of your way," I told the players, "but if he happens to skate by, and gets in your way, give him a tickle." We really weren't that concerned about Kharlamov anyway. Ron Ellis had stopped him cold since the first game. But we were concerned about the referees. The Swede, Dahlberg, was skating at the rink in the afternoon and it seemed like he was going to work. We were wrong. "We just got word from the Swede that he can't make it," Eagleson came by the dressing room to tell me before the game. "He's still sick." The Swede wasn't sick. We knew that. He just choked. He didn't want to work the big game. This left us with Bata and Kompalla. I didn't go out for our team workout before the game, naturally. I stayed in the room calmly drinking six cups of coffee in 20 minutes. Fergie brought back word that all three of our injured defenseman, White, Bergman, and Stapleton, were skating well, and that Dryden looked sharp in the warmup. Good. Let's get on with the game and beat these guys. But, no. These great sportsmen from the Soviet Union let us know exactly how they felt about us at this point. "We can't have the usual pre-game ceremonies," one of their messengers told us. "Not enough time, on account of television." In Canada, the final game had been the big one to exchange gifts. The Russians had given us beautiful Soviet dolls. To reciprocate, we had brought a large totem pole from Canada to be given tonight. Eagleson was seeing red.

"You get back and tell your people that we're going to take this totem pole and bring it to center ice and they'll have to take it or skate around it the whole game," Eagleson told them. The Russians got the message. Somehow, TV found the time, although they eliminated three other presentations we had planned. The opening part of the game was predictable. The German put White and Mahovlich in the penalty box on interference calls in the first three minutes. In the first seven games, only a total of two interference calls had been made. This put the Russians in front 1 to 0 when Yakushev, a helluva player, scored at 3:34, knocking home a rebound. In the next minute, all hell broke loose. The German called interference on Parise, and Jean Paul lost his cool. When he slammed his stick to the ice over the call the German tagged him with a misconduct. In six years of pro hockey Parise has never received a misconduct. This got to him, and he charged Kompalla and threatened to hit him with a two hander. Kompalla cringed, thinking he was going to get the stick, but Parise wasn't going to hit him. Kompalla did the right thing. He threw J.P. out of the game, but it was a terrible call in the first place.

Bedlam now prevailed in the Arena. Our great fans started screaming "Let's go home. Let's go home." I lost my cool worse than J.P. First I reached down, looking for anything I could throw, and fired a little stool from our bench out onto the ice. It shattered all over the place. Then I turned and took Fergie's chair and let that go. Our players were all over the referees on the ice and I wished I could have gotten to them myself. They were blatantly, openly, and without any hesitation, trying to steal the game from us. There was only one thing we could do to make them stop—make them look bad, like we had in the previous games. This is why the chairs went and why I continued the argument as long as I could. I wanted these bastards to think that if they did make one more bad call, I would have one of my players go out and crease one of them with a stick.

The madness must have lasted for ten minutes. In the midst of it I spotted Gresko, standing behind the Russian bench which was only 15 feet from ours. "This is all your fault," I screamed at him. "You asked for this. We told you this would happen if you put that German out there." He was embarrassed. He knew I was right, and like he did when we had him cornered, he just hung his head and looked at the ground. Even before we got back to playing again we had our friendly Red Army back on riot alert. They were now stationed all over the building, shoulder to shoulder, ready for anything. The game got back under way and the Czech gave us a little help. He sent a Russian off for interference—imagine that—and Esposito scored on the power play to tie it up. It was marvelous hockey. Both teams were working hard, giving everything they had in their bodies. The Russians, on another power play, took a 2 to 1 lead at 13:10 on a good shot from the point by Lutchenko. A few minutes later we tied it up again when Park and Ratelle moved beautifully through the Russian zone on a give and go with Brad moving in close to beat Tretiak and finish off a nice play. The first period ended 2 to 2.

On the way back to the dressing room we discovered that the Red Army had our dressing room blocked off like they did the other night. This time I wasn't going to be the nice guy and ask permission to get into my own dressing room. About 20 feet away from this solid wall of uniforms I took off and lowered my shoulder, blasting two of them out of the way with a block before strolling into the room.

Russia moved back in front 3 to 2 as soon as the second period began, on the type of fluke goal we had worried about. Remember that mesh wire fence they have behind the goals here? It gave the Russians a crazy bounce this time, sending a missed shot right back out in front of Dryden when he was looking the other way, making it easy for Shadrin to score. The tempo of the game was still amazing. The crowd noise was deafening. Bill White tied it for us at 10:32 on a pretty play, as he snuck in from the point to take a goalmouth pass from Gilbert and slipped it behind Tretiak into an open corner.

Here, for some unexplainable reason, we stopped skating again as we had in the third period of the first game. In the final ten minutes of the second period the Russians scored twice to go ahead 5 to 3. Yakushev scored again when we left him in front alone on a faceoff. He got a clear shot at Dryden. Then they got their third power play goal of the game and things looked bad for us.

In the dressing room before the third period, we knew what we had to do. "We've got to get one back quickly," I told the players. "But don't gamble to do it. The first ten minutes of this period, we'll concentrate on keeping them from scoring any more. We can't let it get out of reach. In the last ten minutes we can do all the gambling we have to." And like a dream, it all worked! Esposito jammed one by Tretiak from in front in the first three minutes and we were only a goal behind. We were playing hockey again! Each player was concentrating on his man and not making the big mistake. And then, for some reason which I'll never really understand, the Russians, for the first time in seven games, two periods, and ten minutes, changed their game. They went to defense. Instead of pressing like they had without fail, they started to hang back and protect the lead. This opened it up and gave us better chances.

Cournoyer converted one of them at 12:56 to tie the game up as every Canadian in the building, fans and players alike, went wild. Eagleson was one of them, but for another reason. When the Russians didn't put on the red light, he raced to the timer's bench to protest. He was immediately pounced on by a dozen KGB goons who were trying to drag him out of the rink. It was a good thing Peter Mahovlich spotted it, or Al might be getting the cold shower treatment right now. It was on the opposite side of the rink, and they belted Eagleson with some good punches, mostly in the back, before Peter went over the boards and threatened to smash them with his stick. All of us raced across the ice and the Russians backed off. We grabbed Al, who was as white as a sheet, and took him back across the ice to our bench.

He was shaken. I can't say now how much that incident did for us. But it didn't hurt. More than ever, our guys were determined to beat these Russians. They accommodated us by continuing to play defense. We were getting the good chances now. They were willing to accept the tie. We weren't. In the final minute, I wanted to get our best line onto the ice. In my opinion, it had been the Clarke line with Henderson and Ellis. At first I had Ratelle's line up for the last shift, but I changed. Clarke's line was better defensively, and I didn't want to blow the game in the last minute either. With a minute to play Henderson jumped on. But Esposito wouldn't come off. Thank God. Phil had the puck near the Russian net when he rolled a shot in on Tretiak from a difficult angle. The rebound came to Henderson in front. Paul shot, Tretiak saved. The rebound came back and Henderson slid it underneath him. As I remember it now, we didn't believe it for a split second. Our bench seemed to freeze. Maybe it was too good to be true. Suddenly, all the players were over the boards smothering Henderson. I looked at the clock—34 seconds. I thought we had more time left than that, but I wished it were only four. I got the players who were going to be on the ice for the final half minute—Ellis, Espo, Peter—and told them not to take any chances. Just dump the puck out of the zone and keep them at center ice. The Russians never came close. When the game ended, Fergie, Eagleson and I threw our arms around one another and ran across the ice like little kids. It's a wonder we didn't break our necks. I kept telling them, "Never in doubt, was it, fellas?".

Our dressing room was filled with happiness. More than

jubilation, we all felt vindication. We had showed our detractors that when it was all on the line, we could do the job. And we did it our way. There wasn't any champagne at the arena, so we were anxious to get back to the hotel and let it all hang out.

But first we had to stop by the Russian 'victory' party. It was at the Metropole Hotel and all the players from both teams, and their wives, were supposed to attend. The bad guys from Canada showed up, but the good sports from the Soviet Union didn't make it for some strange reason. And it was their party. Only two of their players were there—Yakushev and Tretiak. Yakushev was there to get an award as the best forward in the series. Park got it as the best defenseman. There were a few brief speeches, and Mr. Gresko gave us an idea of how gracious the Soviets are in defeat. Eagleson had spoken first and talked about how he hoped the series had been friendly throughout, despite some of the apparent difficulties. When Gresko had his turn he replied: "I made a friend of Alan Eagleson in July and that friendship lasted until two days ago. Today, and tonight, I feel very sorry for Alan Eagleson." With that he led the Russians out of the room. The Eagle chased him for an explanation, but he kept on coming back with the same bit: "I feel sorry for you". Our attitude is unprintable.

We decided to leave that wake and come here for our own party. It was great. We all let our hair down. Henderson told me at the party that he suffered a groin pull in the first period, and thought he mightn't be able to go on. He never said a word about it during the game. It was also about this time, in thinking back over the game, that I discovered what the Russians were up to at the end. Under international rules, in a series like this, if it ends in a tie, the team with the most goals can proclaim victory for itself. If we tied 5 to 5, they would have had one more goal than us overall and would have made their great pronouncement. This is why they deviated from their style of play near the end and I will always be thankful for that strategy.

Our party has been over for a couple of hours but the players are still going at it pretty good. Every so often a knock comes to the door, and a couple of them are out there, arms around each other with smiles that won't disappear for months.

I'm not going to get any sleep, I can see that. It's just as well.

Our plane takes off at seven this morning and I'll be the first one on it. Tonight, as we left our dressing room at the rink, I walked down the runway to take one final look. The lights were out over the playing surface. The score had been taken down. And in the stands, cleaning women were already about their duties. And when I turned to walk away for the last time, I had the same feeling that I had when I was here in July. The best day in your life is the day you leave this place.

Prague, Sept. 29

How did we beat them? I don't have the answer. I've been thinking a lot about that today, despite this terrible hangover. At least I hope it's a hangover. Maybe those Russians pulled a little germ warfare on me before I got out of that miserable place. I know a few who would have loved to have given me the "shower" treatment.

But as bitter as I am about their lying officials, I have to take my hat off to the Russian players. I don't know how they lost, except that our players outgutted them in the end. But ask yourself this: How did the Russians lose when they can skate as well as us, pass as well as us, take a pass as well as us, play a better team game than us, and outcondition us? The only area in which I thought we were really superior was shooting. (Yet they don't shoot that badly.)

I started thinking about this today on the flight here from Moscow, and the thought kept coming back to me that we won because we knew how to play the big game. A lot of people in sports think the toughest championship to win is the first one. Though this was the first series of this kind for both teams, Canadian pros definitely are more accustomed to playing in games with more at stake than the Russians. Just look at the way we won the last three games, games we couldn't afford to lose. We won them all in the closing minutes. At the start of the series, you would have said that Russia would win any games decided in the final minutes because their team would be stronger because of their great conditioning. They were stronger physically, but we were tougher mentally. Our mental conditioning—the kind of toughness that comes only from playing in something like the Stanley Cup—is the thing that, in the end, proved the difference. This came to me as I was sitting in the midst of our wild party on the plane. The boys still had their vodka handy, and some of them didn't bother to sleep at all.

We were supposed to have practiced today but the hell with it. I want the guys to let it all hang out. They've earned it. I look at a guy like Paul Henderson and I think from the very first day of training camp, he's never had a bad practice or game. He came here to prove he can play with any one in hockey, and he did. The guys on his line, Ellis and Clarke, were just as dedicated. Ellis hasn't said two words since we put this team together, but Ron has been our best defensive forward. We put him on Kharlamov, one of the best players in the world, and Ellis grudgingly gave him one goal over the final seven games.

Look at what the Espositos did for us. Tony would get so psyched for these games, he'd come into the dressing room like he just got run over by a truck, walking around like a zombie. You never saw a player look so bewildered before a game. But once the whistle blew he hung tough. I'm very happy for Phil. In Chicago he played in Bobby Hull's shadow. In Boston, he's got to live with Bobby Orr. After this series, Phil Esposito will stand only in his own shadow, one of the best that ever laced up a pair of skates.

I'm just as happy for Parise. Jean-Paul isn't a good scorer, but he can do everything else. He came up to me today and told me, "If we had lost that game on account of what I did I would have killed myself." He's such a great competitor he probably would have.

We were lucky we had a lot of class on this team. It's easy to play when you're doing well. When you're not doing well and you're still grinding, then you've got heart. I put Cournoyer, Ratelle and Gilbert in this category. All three knew they weren't in top form against the Russians, but they kept going. And as it turned out they got us some big goals.

The two Mahovlichs are like day and night. Big Frank has been quiet, distant. He keeps within himself, yet he was always 100 percent behind everything about this operation. Peter . . . well, Peter is beautiful. He's the clown prince of our team. When things got hairy, he always had something to say that kept our wit and our wits about us.

Just the opposite is Ken Dryden. You get very little out of Dryden. He's a guy who likes to analyze every game to the nth degree.

Brad Park didn't have a great series, for Brad Park. His forte is anticipating passes, moving up to intercept, and then making a play. He couldn't do this against the Russians, who were constantly getting behind him in the early games. But Brad kept his poise, carried the puck well, and in the final game gave us a super performance.

His partner Gary Bergman was probably the biggest surprise on the team. When we picked Gary we never in our wildest dreams thought he would contribute so much.

Bill White was the same way, no big advance notices, just a solid, stand up defenseman who played as well at his position as anyone we had. We scared hell out of Bill this morning. We left the hotel at seven o'clock and it was the first time—because of all the confusion—that we couldn't check that we had everyone on the buses. We were out at the airport for an hour (our plane was late leaving) when Bill arrived, white as a ghost. "I'm scared to death," he told me. "I thought you guys had left me behind." None of our players relished the idea of staying behind.

Bill's partner Whitey Stapleton is a grand little guy. Great consistency, does his job and never takes himself too seriously. One day after our defectors had gone home, Whitey came up to me and said: 'Harry, I'm leaving. You promised me I could have a holiday somewhere in this series and I've had to play every damn game. That's too much. I'm getting out of here."

We have plenty of guys on this team who didn't get much—some none—ice time, and who still hung tough with us. Perhaps by now they hate my guts for not letting them play more, but in my heart I will always have a special affection for Don Awrey, Rod Seiling, Wayne Cashman, Bill Goldsworthy, Stan Mikita, Red Berenson, Dale Tallon, Marcel Dionne, Brian Glennie, Eddie Johnston and Dennis Hull. They're stars in their own right, and I made them sit on the bench. If they disliked it—and they had to—they never threw it up at me. This crew nicknamed themselves "The Goons" but they certainly never acted that way.

By now it's obvious that I'm looking down my roster trying to reflect on every guy, and I've deliberately left two till last—Savard and Lapointe. They are special. Savard was belittled in some areas when he was selected for the squad. He reinjured his ankle early, but he shook off a fracture to come to Europe even when it was doubtful he could play. And how did he play? He is the only guy on the team who played in every winning game and no losing games.

Lapointe is just a young kid, but he's a real man. His wife was expecting their first child when we left Canada, and no one wants to be away from an event like that. She had the baby while we were in Sweden and today Guy flew to Canada instead of coming here. But he waited until he fulfilled his commitment before leaving.

One thing I'd like to add before I hit the sack, (and I'm going to right away because I feel terrible) is a mention of two passengers on our flight today—old friends of ours. Guess who was sitting up in first class, side by side, exchanging niceties? Coach Bobrov and Kompalla, the German referee. We thought it only fitting that we send some Canadian representatives to keep them company. Cashman and Peter Mahovlich volunteered and I understand the four lunched together. Someday I'll have to get the complete details.

Prague, Sept. 30

I'm not getting any healthier, but I am getting more brilliant with each game, if that's possible. Tonight I once again amazed even myself with my brilliant late game strategy. After bailing out of defeat for the fourth time in a week in the final minutes, I must concede that old Lady Luck is all over me. I mean, lately she's really had a crush on old Harry J.

In this game with the Czechs, we were losing 3 to 2 in the final 10 seconds and it looked like we were gone. Believe me when I tell you I was mad about it because I never wanted to play here in the first place, and because a loss would have taken some of the gloss off our great victory in Russia. I pulled the goalie, Dryden, and we're going with six skaters when I decided to try something new. I got all our big strong guys together and told them just to go for the net—Phil Esposito, Savard, Pete Mahovlich. Phil didn't like this idea because he wants to take the faceoff in their end of the rink. "I've beaten this guy on every faceoff tonight. I can beat him now." he said.

I told Phil: "You probably can, but I want Bobby Clarke to take the faceoff. He's as good as we got and I want you to be in the slot. Tell Bobby to get the puck to Brad Park on the point. And tell Brad to get a shot on net—but to keep it low. We want one of you big guys in front to get the rebound and bang it home."

Well, on the draw Clarke gets it to Park, who shot, but not that hard, and it was tied up in the crease. With seven seconds left we tried it all over again. Clarke won the draw. Park got more wood on the puck this time and drilled it on net. Our big boys were camped on the doorstep, and Savard stuffed it in to tie the game at 3 to 3 with just four seconds to play. We stole another one. What did I say about the Canadians knowing how to make the big play?

The Czechs are good. Better than the Swedes, but not as good as the Russians. They should have beaten us, though. In the first period we jumped out in front 2 to 0 because they suffered the same malady the Swedes did our first game with them—awe. The Czechs couldn't keep their feet on the ground in the first period. Savard and Peter popped in goals for us and we had a 2 to 0 lead. Dryden was in net and although we planned to split the game with Tony, Ken had a shutout going and we decided to give him a crack at it.

After the first period it was all the Czechs. Like the Swedes and Russians, they wanted a victory over us badly. We were supposed to have the German, Kompalla, referee tonight, but he thought better of it and begged off. He must have come down with the same kind of bug that afflicted the Swede, Dahlberg, in Russia before our last game.

So we ended up playing the Czechs with three of their countrymen officiating. (Three because they used the NHL system—and it *was* better, despite some decided signs of patriotism on the part of the men in the striped shirts.) The fortunate thing is that we got out without losing, and that was our goal.

Fergie and I had to make some tough decisions before this one. We had promised that everyone on Team Canada would play in some game along the way. In Russia we hardly used any of the "Goons" and we wanted them to play against the Czechs. "Listen," Fergie told me, "these guys are all stars in the NHL and they should be good enough to handle any Czech national team." We went with the "Goons" and got away with it. I think if they had had their legs, and played their pace for three periods, we would have won.

In one way, it was a very nice evening for us. It was homecoming for Stan Mikita, a real pro. Stan left

Czechoslovakia when he was eight and his mother sent him to live in Canada with an aunt and uncle. During the years his family was still behind the Iron Curtain, Stan kept in touch. When he made the big leagues he sent money to his mother regularly and never forgot his people. Stan didn't stay for our final game in Russia. I told him to take off and see his mother here a day early, which is what he wanted to do. We made Stan captain tonight and when he was introduced, he got the greatest ovation of any player on either squad. He was out there for the opening faceoff and just missed scoring a goal.

I was very sick myself during the game. The doctor took my temperature and it was 102. This forced me to come right back to the hotel after the game and jump into bed. They've got a big reception waiting for us in Canada tomorrow and I've got to get myself together.

Our trip home actually started tonight, in a scene I will never forget. When the game was over, and all the players filed into the dressing room, we realized that this was the last time, perhaps forever, Team Canada would be together as a group. No one said anything, but you could sense a nostalgic feeling vibrating among the players. For the first few minutes they went about putting away their gear methodically, somberly. Then someone started humming a song; I'm pretty sure it was Phil Esposito. Then he started to sing it: "Thanks for the Memories," Bob Hope's theme song. And almost like it had been rehearsed, every guy stood in front of his locker, stopped for a few minutes, and joined in as loudly as he could. It lacked quality, but it had heart.

And right down to the end, the last thing they would do together as a team abounded with the greatest attribute of this squad: Heart.

Toronto, Oct. 1,
This has been a day of high emotion for me, the players, and all of Canada. The villains of seven days ago are now the conquering heroes. It was a long day, starting in Prague with a tearful scene at our hotel and finishing here in front of city hall with raindrops falling gloriously on our heads, washing away most of the ill will that had afflicted Team Canada from time to time.

But some resentment will always stick with the people of

Team Canada. We were thrown to the wolves, set up as the bad guys. We found many people we thought were friends kicking us when we were down. And then we came back to beat perhaps the finest hockey team in the world on their terms, on their ice. As much as we appreciated the tumultuous welcome we received today in Montreal and here, we know that part of the legacy from this adventure will be severe and continuing criticism from our detractors.

I feel sorry for these people. I know many of them, and they all have one thing in common—they're losers. And they'll be losers all their lives. I feel sorry for them because the easiest thing to do in a bad situation is quit. These are the fans, the writers, the former players and coaches who picked us to win eight straight and then started tearing our players apart when the Russians proved much tougher than anyone ever anticipated. Why didn't they give the Russians credit? We did. But no; that would have meant admitting they were wrong, that the NHL's best really weren't the supreme masters of the game. So instead of praising the Russians, they started chipping away at us, cutting us up from behind when the toughest fight of our lives was in front of us.

But like I said, almost all of that rancor has left us. We're just keeping some of it with us as another lesson well learned in life.

Our players wanted to get home in the worst way. We assembled early to catch our buses at the hotel in Prague and sat by sadly as Stan Mikita's mom sobbed uncontrollably when we were leaving. It was very moving and loving. I had the feeling that Stan's mom felt she was never going to see her son again. It was that kind of scene. I couldn't make the banquet the Czechs gave for us last night because I was sick. The guys told me that Stan gave a tremendous speech in his native tongue. Today we are all very proud that Stan Mikita is our teammate.

The flight home was long and tedious. All those hours on the plane, going through those time zones, really beats hell out of you. I started to feel better about half way home. The players were happy. Many of them played cards and all of them talked excitedly of the big crowds that were supposed to be waiting for us. These guys have all been honored many times before, but they knew that what was ahead would be totally different, a once in a lifetime experience.

The past two days I had said most of my "thank yous" to the players. On the ride back I wanted to spend time with my great friends of Team Five. Bobby Haggert, who handled the logistics of moving us from Toronto to Montreal to Winnipeg to Vancouver to Stockholm to Moscow to Prague without a hitch, was the guy who always had the joke or the good line when things got too serious. Mike Cannon was just as efficient with all the visa and player problems we encountered along the way, and they were numerous.

In front of me on the plane, sitting side by side, were Al Eagleson and John Ferguson. Gresco might have felt sorry for Al, but I'm very glad for him. He, more than anyone else, should take the bows for Team Canada. Al's the guy who put it all together. The series saved the life of Hockey Canada and added greatly to the player pension fund. When the going got tough, Eagleson stood in front and stuck his chin out in more ways than one. Al may have a short fuse, but he's long on loyalty. He never wavered once, no matter what the controversy. When Fergie and I needed backing, he was always there, even if it meant fighting for us.

So don't knock Al Eagleson to me, or you might find I've suddenly developed a short fuse. I'd like to see how his critics would have fared in his situation in Russia. None of us ever wanted this series to deteriorate the way it did. Al was the last guy who wanted any trouble. Never forget that in Russia the Soviets set the tempo. We just decided not to dance to their music.

About half an hour out of Montreal I moved up to say my goodbyes to John Ferguson. John and I really didn't have to say anything to one another. What we felt didn't have to be transmitted by words. As we started to talk I saw his eyes filling up, the tears forming in the corners. I got all choked up and had to walk away. I went to the back of the plane and wanted to cry. If I were alone, I would have.

There is just no way to measure what John Ferguson did for me and for this team. He was the only guy who never said die. He would never let anyone think about losing. He just wouldn't allow it. During the series he was knocked in the papers as a guy who didn't have enough experience to hold a sensitive coaching position. But John Ferguson is a great coach. In the beginning I picked John because I knew he is in the Toe Blake tradition and that he thought a great deal of

Blake and his methods in the years they were together on those great Montreal teams. Toe Blake should be proud of John Ferguson. As far as I'm concerned, John took that tradition to its greatest heights during this series.

I gave John the dirtiest jobs. I always took the happy guys, the ones going to play, to practice. He had to take the "Goons," find a way to make them practice hard, and keep them happy at the same time. He did, and they respected him. On the bench he was great. He kept our players fired up every time they went over the boards for a new shift. Countless times he came to me with good tips and astute observations about the Soviet style of play and the trends in a particular game.

Many times in the latter stages of the series I wished I could have had John playing for me. We would have straightened out the Russians a lot sooner. They wouldn't have been as quick to spear or kick. If one of them pulled that on John, he would have had a forced fed meal of Canadian hockey stick, followed by a few Canadian knuckle sandwiches. But in street shoes, John Ferguson is not that type. He is a beautiful person. My greatest benefit from this series will be knowing how fortunate I am to have made such a great friend.

I didn't talk to John again on the flight. It would have embarrassed both of us to start crying at each other. He was getting off the plane in Montreal with seven of the players. The rest of us would go on to Toronto and the big reception here.

In Montreal, Mayor Drapeau was at the airport to greet us. All of Team Canada got off the plane and toured the airport on fire engines. The sun was out and the crowd was warm.

As I went back up the stairs to the plane, I looked back to see if I could find John in the crowd. I saw him standing beside one of the fire engines staring up at me. It was too noisy to shout anything, so I just brought up my hand and gave him a little salute. He nodded back at me with a slight smile. I turned quickly and went into the plane. My eyes were getting watery and it took a dozen good, deep breaths to hold back that part of me that wanted to explode into tears. I don't think it's possible for a man to feel more for another man than I do for John Ferguson.

We were late reaching Toronto. It was dark and raining very hard. At the airport I was surprised to see my mother and my sister Betty. Some kind person had been considerate enough to bring them. I was looking for my wife, Eleanor, but I couldn't find her. I wanted all the Sinden girls to be in on this one. My mom was thrilled. "Too bad your dad isn't alive to see you now," she told me. I had the same thought myself.

All the way in from the airport we could see cars filled with happy Canadians parked along the road, waving at us as their windshield wipers sloshed away the rain. Our caravan went right to city hall and into a parking garage. When all of the players and Team Canada officials were together, they took us upstairs to a huge platform overlooking 80,000 of our countrymen who had stood in the rain for hours, waiting.

When it came my turn to say something, I really didn't have the appropriate words. I asked the crowd to have one more "Nyet, nyet, Soviet! Da, da, Canada!" the cheer our fans had concocted in Russia. The crowd here followed suit.

As I stepped back the crowd continued to salute the players, and I realized that what I wanted most for these players was happening right in front of me. I wanted them to experience the indescribable thrill of winning for their country. That was my wish. It has been granted. Go into their heart 10 years from now and I think they'll tell you the greatest moment they ever lived through came tonight, when all those people stood soaking wet to sing O Canada for them.

Thanks for the memories.